Ethical Insights
A Brief Introduction

Douglas Birsch

Shippensburg University of Pennsylvania

Mayfield Publishing Company

Mountain View, California
London • Toronto

To my ethics students,
past, present, and future,
and to my first ethics professor, Dr. James F. Sheridan

Library of Congress Cataloging-in-Publication Data

Birsch, Douglas
    Ethical insights : a brief introduction / Douglas Birsch.
        p.   cm.
    ISBN 0-7674-0712-1
    1. Ethics.   I. Title.
BJ1025.B54   1998
171—dc21   98-27070
                                                                              CIP

Manufactured in the United States of America
10   9   8   7   6   5   4   3   2   1

Mayfield Publishing Company
1280 Villa Street
Mountain View, CA 94041

Sponsoring editor, Kenneth King; production editor, Julianna Scott Fein; manuscript editor, Kay C. Mikel; design manager and cover designer, Susan Breitbard;
text designer, Claire Seng-Niemoeller; manufacturing manager, Randy Hurst.
The text was set in 10/12.5 Garth Graphic by TBH Typecast, Inc. and printed on
acid-free 50# Finch Opaque by Malloy Lithographing, Inc.

Preface

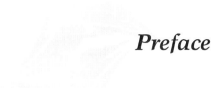

Ethical Insights is a concise introduction to ethics and ethical theories. Its purpose is to provide students with the conceptual framework to facilitate thoughtful and profitable discussions of ethical problems. It is designed as a supplemental book for applied ethics classes, such as classes in contemporary moral issues, bioethics, business ethics, computer ethics, engineering ethics, or environmental ethics.

Organization

Ethical Insights contains a general introduction to ethics (Chapter 1), six short chapters on ethical theories, and a final chapter exploring a pluralistic approach to ethics. The book is organized around ethical insights, traditional ethical assumptions, and four ethical themes. (Appendix 1 provides a summary of these three elements.) The chapters on ethical theories have a common pattern:

- identification of the ethical insight related to the theory;
- the theory's ethical standard, which establishes moral guidelines to help solve ethical problems;
- analysis of the theory in terms of the traditional ethical assumptions and the four basic ethical themes discussed in Chapter 1;
- comparison with another theory, usually the one in the preceding chapter;
- some of the problems that emerge with the theory;
- appraisal of the theory in terms of the criteria for a successful ethical theory presented in Chapter 1; and
- questions to help the reader review key concepts.

I have chosen not to include some of the subtleties of the ethical theories so that the instructor can spend the bulk of the course discussing ethical problems rather than explaining the intricacies of Kant's ideas or hedonistic utilitarianism. Because this book is designed for use in a variety of applied ethics courses, I have also deliberately omitted case studies. Including such material for each type of course would have excessively lengthened the text.

The Ethical Theories

I have chosen to label the approaches to ethics in this book "ethical theories." In Chapter 1 I provide two functional definitions: (1) ethical theories provide clear and reasonable concepts to use in responding to ethical problems, and (2) ethical theories identify the legitimate moral guidelines that can help us solve ethical problems and live together successfully. The approaches to ethics discussed in the subsequent chapters can be viewed as "theories" because they attempt to accomplish these functions.

The six moral theories presented in this book are versions of ethical relativism, act utilitarianism, Kantian ethics, the moral rights theory, virtue ethics, and the ethic of care. These theories center, respectively, on social moral principles, harm and benefit for morally significant beings, consistency and moral equality, moral rights, the virtues, and care.

I have chosen these six theories because they are the ones that I have used most profitably in my classes, perhaps because the insights related to each of them make sense to students. This is crucial for me. I want to provide a conceptual ethical framework for the course using theories that are related to familiar insights. Several of the theories (act utilitarianism, the moral rights theory, and virtue ethics) also contain familiar moral vocabularies, such as harm and benefit, rights, and virtues.

My choices of ethical relativism, act utilitarianism, and Kantian ethics are probably not particularly controversial, but possibly the other selections may require some explanation. I have included a chapter on moral rights because I believe that we can produce a plausible "ethical theory" centered around moral rights, and I personally prefer discussing moral rights as a representative deontological theory rather than the more common choice, Kant's ethical theory. Because contemporary moral problems are often discussed in the language of rights, most students are familiar with the key concepts, and, in my experience, they find rights easier to understand and more interesting than the various formulations of the Categorical Imperative. Although I prefer the moral rights theory, many other professors prefer Kantian ethics as a representative deontological theory, so I have included a chapter on Kantian ethics. This gives the instructor the option of using one or both chapters.

I chose virtue ethics, or more precisely Aristotle's ethics, because it allows the instructor to develop the idea of ethics in terms of a goal, purpose, or function—in Aristotle's case, a universal human purpose. Aristotle's theory can form the foundation for a discussion of organizational ethics in terms of the goals, purposes, or functions of corporations and organizations, an approach I find especially useful in business ethics. Inclusion of virtue ethics allows both exploration of the concept of virtue in general and discussion of specific virtues. Moreover, like the moral rights theory, virtue ethics has a familiar moral vocabulary, such as courage, generosity, and friendliness.

The last and probably most controversial choice is Nel Noddings's version of the ethic of care. I included this theory because it provides a contemporary rejection of many of the traditional ethical ideas, such as universalizability and moral equality. If the instructor is sympathetic to the claim that men and women have different ways of talking about ethics, this theory can also be used to represent a feminine approach to solving moral problems.

Suggestions for Using This Book

Ethical Insights can be used at the beginning of the course to introduce students to ethics and ethical theories and to prepare them for subsequent discussions of ethical problems. A second way to use the book is to integrate the appropriate chapters into the discussion of moral problems or issues. For instance, students could read the chapter on moral rights before discussing the abortion issue.

This book is intended to make the task of teaching ethical theories in applied ethics classes easier. Ethical theories are difficult for many students to understand; unlike ethical problems, they can seem abstract and remote from the students' experience. I think this book responds to this concern.

Acknowledgments

Many people helped to make this book possible, especially Ken King, the philosophy editor at Mayfield. Also at Mayfield, I am grateful to Josh Tepfer, editorial assistant; Julianna Scott Fein, production editor; Susan Breitbard, design manager; and Kay Mikel, copyeditor. I am also grateful to the reviewers: Dasiea Cavers-Huff, Riverside Community College; Dawn Jakubowski, University of Kansas; Joan McGregor, Arizona State University; Levonne Nelson, Fullerton College; and David C. Ring, Long Beach City College. At and around home, I appreciate the efforts of

Ellen Birsch, Dr. John Fielder, Olivia Yeung, Kathryn Birsch, Jocelyn Birsch, and Jan Birsch. At Shippensburg University, I received assistance from Toby Watkins, Dr. Jim Coolsen, Shirley Mellinger, Robyn Burns, Brad Linard, Jason Lukach, Rachel Varner, Matt Seeley, and Barb Wheeler. A special thank you is due to Dr. Charles Loucks, who edited the entire manuscript.

Contents

Preface   iii

CHAPTER 1 / **An Introduction to Ethics and Ethical Theories**   1

Ethics, Theoretical Ethics, and Applied Ethics   2
Alternative Sources of Solutions   3
Ethical Theories   5
Evaluating Ethical Theories   6
Some Traditional Assumptions of Ethical Theories   7
   Rationality   7
   Moral Equals   8
   Universalizability   10
Basic Themes Associated with Ethics   10
Conclusion   13
Questions for Review   13
Notes   14

CHAPTER 2 / **Ethical Relativism**   15

Ethical Relativism and Ethical Subjectivism   15
One Version of Ethical Relativism   17
Ethical Relativism and Tolerance   18
Justification and Determining the Morally Significant   20
Ethical Relativism and the Traditional Ethical Assumptions   21
Ethical Relativism and the Four Basic Ethical Themes   22
Problems with Ethical Relativism   23
   Actual Ethical Guidelines   24
   Multiple Sets of Ethical Guidelines   26
   Moral Progress and Dissent   27
Conclusion   28
Questions for Review   28
Notes   29

CHAPTER 3 / **Act Utilitarianism**   31

Act Utilitarianism and Ethical Egoism   31
The Essential Principle and Standard of Act Utilitarianism   33
Benefit and Harm   34
Justification and Determining the Morally Significant   35
Amendments to the Original Insight   36
Act Utilitarian Calculations   37
Act Utilitarianism and the Traditional Ethical Assumptions   39
Act Utilitarianism and the Basic Ethical Themes   40
Contrasting Act Utilitarianism with Ethical Relativism   41
Problems with Act Utilitarianism   42
   Doing the Calculations   42
   Injustice   44
   Moral Luck   45
Rule Utilitarianism   46
Conclusion   48
Questions for Review   49
Notes   50

CHAPTER 4 / **Kantian Ethical Theory**   51

Rules and Action   52
The Basic Ethical Insights of Kantian Ethics   52
Persons and Moral Laws   53
The Ethical Standard of Kantian Ethics   54
Legitimate Moral Laws   55
Justification and Determining the Morally Significant   57
Kantian Ethics and the Traditional Ethical Assumptions   58
Kantian Ethics and the Four Ethical Themes   59
Contrasting Kantian Ethics with Act Utilitarianism   60
Problems with Kantian Ethics   60
   Descriptions for Actions   61
   Conflicting Moral Laws   61
   Exceptions to Moral Laws   62
Conclusion   63
Questions for Review   63
Notes   64

CHAPTER 5 / **The Moral Rights Theory**   65

Who Has Moral Rights?   66
Moral Rights and Duties   67

Basic Rights   68
  Life   68
  Well-Being   68
  Liberty   69
  Privacy   69
  Property   70
An Alternative View of Moral Rights   71
Justification and Determining the Morally Significant   72
Moral Rights and the Traditional Ethical Assumptions   72
Moral Rights and the Basic Ethical Themes   73
Contrasting Moral Rights with Act Utilitarianism   74
Problems with the Theory   75
  Descriptions of Actions   75
  Conflicting Rights   76
  The Community   77
Conclusion   78
Questions for Review   78
Notes   79

CHAPTER 6 / **Virtue Ethics**   81

Virtue Ethics, Well-Being, and Reasoning   82
Intellectual Virtues   83
Moral Virtues and Vices   84
Justification and Determining the Morally Significant   86
Virtue Ethics and the Traditional Ethical Assumptions   87
Virtue Ethics and the Four Ethical Themes   88
Differences Between Virtue Ethics and the Moral
  Rights Theory   89
Problems with Virtue Ethics   90
  Lack of Effective Ethical Guidelines   90
  Moral Luck   91
  The Fundamental Human Function   92
Conclusion   93
Questions for Review   93
Notes   94

CHAPTER 7 / **The Ethic of Care**   95

The Background to Noddings's Theory   95
Natural and Ethical Caring   97
Ethical Obligation and the Ethical Ideal   98

The Ethical Standard of the Ethic of Care   98
The Limit of Ethical Caring and the Morally Significant   99
Justification for the Ethical Standard   100
The Ethic of Care and the Traditional Ethical Assumptions   101
The Ethic of Care and the Four Ethical Themes   101
Some Differences Between the Ethic of Care
    and Virtue Ethics   102
Problems with the Ethic of Care   103
    Incomplete Moral Standard   103
    Exploitation of the One-Caring   104
    Limits on Promoting Welfare   105
Conclusion   106
Questions for Review   106
Notes   107

CHAPTER 8 / **A Pluralistic View of Ethics**   109

Moral Communities and Loyalty   110
Full-Scale Morally Significant Beings   111
Large Moral Communities   114
Intermediate Moral Communities   116
Small Moral Communities   117
Moral Communities and Conflicting Moral Obligations   118
Misguided Loyalty to a Moral Community   120
Conclusion   121
Questions for Review   122
Notes   123

APPENDIX 1   125

APPENDIX 2   127

Index   133

Chapter 1

An Introduction to Ethics and Ethical Theories

All of us face ethical problems from time to time. These problems turn up in relation to most human activities. Sustaining friendships, raising children, selling things, or providing others with information can present us with serious dilemmas that have serious consequences. Some ethical problems that could confront any college student are described in the following paragraphs. The descriptions of the problems are brief, so as you read about them, think about what additional information would be helpful for resolving them.

You are friends with two people involved in a serious relationship. You find out that one of them is cheating on the other. Should you tell the deceived person? Why, or why not? Suppose the deceived person asks you about the matter. Should you lie or tell the truth?

You need a textbook for a very important class but lack the money to buy it. Should you steal the textbook from the bookstore if you believe there is only a slight chance you would get caught? If you are too scared to steal it from the bookstore, should you steal it from a wealthy friend if you believe that he or she would never find out? Why did you give the answers that you did?

You are in your first year of college, and you (or your girlfriend) become pregnant. Would you get an abortion? Would you try to convince your girlfriend to get an abortion? Why, or why not?

You need to get a good grade on the final to pass a class, but you are not confident that you will be successful. Should you cheat on the test if there is almost no chance of getting caught? Why, or why not?

For many years you have been in a serious relationship with another person. Then he or she ends it. You become very depressed and think about killing yourself. Would you try to kill yourself? Why or why not?

You have been paralyzed from the neck down in a car accident. Your life is filled with pain and humiliation. Would you ask a family member or close friend to kill you? Why, or why not?

You are in a relationship with another person. You love this person, and he or she loves you. Now another person (better looking, richer, smarter, more fun) tells you that he or she loves you. Should you break up with the first person and get involved with this new individual? Why, or why not?

Which of these problems seems most serious to you? Was it hard to arrive at answers to these questions? Do you think everyone would agree with your responses? Would you be able to convince people who disagreed with you that you were right and that they were wrong? Do you think it is a good idea to learn more about problems like these and how to solve them?

If you had trouble answering these questions, this book will help you. Each of the next six chapters discusses and evaluates a particular ethical theory. Ethical theories identify legitimate ethical guidelines. These guidelines are tools we can use to help solve ethical problems. Each theory claims that its guidelines are the best tools to use in solving all ethical problems. However, just as we use different tools for different jobs—such as a wrench and not a hammer to loosen a bolt—different sets of ethical guidelines are the optimum tools for particular areas of ethics (See Chapter 8 for more on this topic).

Ethics, Theoretical Ethics, and Applied Ethics

Moral philosophers try to understand and solve ethical problems. If the problems are serious and a great deal rests on their solution, then the task of moral philosophers is an important one. To accomplish this task, philosophers use a variety of conceptual and theoretical ethical resources. This investigation into the conceptual and theoretical ethical resources for solving ethical problems and into the solutions to them is called *ethics*.[1] Ethics is subdivided into *theoretical ethics,* which studies the conceptual and theoretical resources for solving problems, and *applied ethics,* which examines specific problems and offers solutions to them. Ethics discussions traditionally have centered around books and essays written by famous philosophers and other thinkers, but ethics is open to everyone. If you thought about the brief sketches that raised some common ethical problems, you have already started to participate in it.

In the past, theoretical ethics has concentrated on ethical theories. Ethical theories try to answer a variety of questions. How ought we to live? Is it possible to find a rational answer to the question about how we ought to live? What is the difference between good and evil? What makes an action or a belief morally good? Is anything always good or evil? When is a person morally responsible for something? What is virtue in general? What is a particular virtue, and how do these particular virtues relate to virtue in general? What ought we to do or to believe? Why should we act morally?

The answers to these theoretical ethical questions help us do applied ethics and solve ethical problems. Ethical problems come in two forms: (1) specific cases where we must determine the good or right thing to do, say, or believe, and (2) general problems where we attempt to discover the appropriate response to a class or set of actions, statements, or beliefs. Finding successful solutions to ethical problems is a serious challenge and is of great importance.

Alternative Sources of Solutions

One way to get help in solving ethical problems is to learn about ethical theories, but there are other sources of help as well. *Religion* provides guidelines about how to live and can help us solve these problems. If I am a Christian, my religion informs me about how I ought to live— for example, to follow the Ten Commandments or the Golden Rule. Although religion does inform us about how we ought to live, religious answers are separate from ethical ones. Ethics is open to everyone, no matter what their particular religious beliefs may be, and serious problems arise when we do not separate ethics from religion.

If we claim that God creates good and evil, we would not be able to separate ethics and religion. One way to understand this view is to assert that what is good is what God commands us to do, and what is bad is what God orders us not to do. Now let's look at a few of the problems related to this view. One problem is our inability to resolve the dispute over what text contains the divine commandments. Do we look at the Koran? the Bhagavad Gita? the Bible? the Torah? or some other religious text?

The second problem involves not being able to agree on how to interpret the text that we choose. For example, scholars disagree about the correct interpretation of many passages in the Bible. Does God command us never to divorce our spouses, or is divorce permitted? Does "thou shalt not kill" permit some kinds of killing, and if so, what kinds?

A third problem is that if the only thing that makes something good is that God has commanded it, then good is arbitrary. Suppose that instead of relying on the angel of death God had commanded Moses to kill all the firstborn Egyptian children. Following God's command, Moses murders all these innocent children. If I claimed that these murders were horrible, a religious person would probably tell me that God had a reason for giving this command. The religious person might add that these deaths led to a greater good—the freedom of the Jewish people. If slaying the Egyptian children was good, it was not good simply because God commanded it but because of some other factor, like freeing the Jewish people. If good was only connected to God's commands, then killing the Egyptian children would be good even if it was totally arbitrary (that is, done for no reason at all). Therefore, if good is not to be arbitrary, there must be some view of good and evil that is independent of God.

A fourth problem with the "divine command" view is that it makes very odd the usual claim that God is perfectly good. If good simply means "commanded by God," then "God is perfectly good" means "God is perfectly commanded by God," which is an odd claim to make.

The view that ethics is nonreligious does not deny the existence of God. Actually, it helps make sense out of the claim that God is perfectly good. Keeping ethics and religion separate allows us to avoid these difficult problems and keep the ethical investigation open to everyone, whatever his or her particular religious beliefs.

Laws also inform us about how we ought to live. Some laws are related to ethical problems, but legal considerations are not the same as ethical ones.[2] Laws are rules of conduct established by governments or legislative bodies and usually are connected to specific penalties or punishments. Ethical principles can be created by anyone, and they have no specific penalties attached to them. "Obey the laws" is an ethical claim about how one ought to live, but the laws themselves are legislative rules, not ethical principles. The distinction between laws and morality is reinforced by the possibility that there can be unethical laws.[3] At one time slavery was legal in the United States, but most of us would claim that slavery has always been unethical and that the laws permitting it were immoral ones. The subject of ethics will also be clearer if we maintain this distinction between laws and ethical principles.

What might be called *attitudes* or *relationships* can also provide insight into how we ought to live and can help us solve ethical problems. Love, caring, and friendship shape our daily lives. Traditionally, these attitudes or relationships have not found a central role in ethics because they were thought to be contrary to the search for universalizable ethical guidelines. In my view, however, love, caring, and friendship are ethically significant and, therefore, ethics is more than the search for these universalizable ethical guidelines. In Chapter 7, I will discuss an ethical view centered on caring, and in Chapter 8 I will briefly discuss the importance of special treatment for friends and loved ones.

Ethical Theories

I have chosen to call the approaches to ethics contained in this book "ethical theories." *Ethical theories* provide clear and reasonable concepts to use in responding to ethical problems. More specifically, they provide three things: (1) standards for determining good and evil or right and wrong, (2) justifications for using these particular standards, and (3) differentiations between what is and what is not morally significant. Most of the proponents of ethical theories are distressed by the profusion of ethical beliefs and competing solutions to ethical problems. They believe that their particular approach to ethics is the best one, in the sense that it will furnish the legitimate ethical standard to determine good and evil.

Although many ethical theorists emphasize the previous aspect of ethical theories, there is another one. I agree with Mary Midgley who says:

> Human beings are not limpets or even crocodiles, they are highly social creatures. Except for a few natural hermits, they have to interact fairly constantly if they are to have any sort of a satisfying life. And these interactions are only possible where there is some measure of agreement on basic patterns.[4]

Human beings are indeed social creatures. We live together in societies, and if we are to do so successfully, we must live within certain basic guidelines. Laws provide some of these guidelines and help us to live together successfully, but at least two kinds of situations arise where the laws are insufficient and where we also need ethical guidelines. One situation is illustrated by the slavery example, wherein a law treats one segment of society unfairly or harmfully. An ethical standard allows us to evaluate the questionable law. Another situation arises when society would run more smoothly if people acted in a certain way, but the law is inadequate to produce the desired actions. In general, we believe we can get along better if we do not steal each other's property. Imagine that you find a wallet containing a hundred dollars in a deserted area at night. No one is nearby. You could take the hundred dollars, discard the wallet, and have no reason to fear being caught and punished. However, if you were guided by the moral principle that it is wrong to steal other people's property, you would return the wallet. We get along better if people return wallets and if property is protected. Thus, ethical guidelines help us live together more successfully. The second aspect of ethical theories is that they identify ethical guidelines that can help us live together more successfully.

Ethical theories identify moral guidelines. These guidelines create a view of ethical activity that contrasts with the unlimited pursuit of self-interest. If people believe that it is permissible to do anything that is in their self-interest, they may injure other individuals or society in general to benefit themselves. This will interfere with living together successfully. Ethical theories help to prevent injury to individuals and to society by identifying a view of "good" that opposes the unlimited pursuit of self-interest. This does not mean that ethical people can never act in their own self-interest, only that there are limitations on the pursuit of self-interest.

In my opinion, the most important function of ethical theories is to identify moral guidelines that can help us solve ethical problems and live together successfully. The two aspects of this function are closely related. Ethical problems usually involve other people. Should I tell the deceived friend the truth? Should I steal the textbook? Should I end the relationship? The solutions to these ethical problems will affect how successfully we can live with others.

Evaluating Ethical Theories

The most important function of ethical theories is to identify legitimate moral guidelines to help us solve ethical problems and to help us live together more successfully. In this book, I will evaluate the ethical theories presented in relation to their success at accomplishing this function. Here are the criteria I will use for this evaluation:

1. The ethical theory must be able to identify some ethical guidelines.

2. The theory must be able to show that some ethical guidelines are better than others. (A theory that concludes that any ethical guideline is as good as any other would legitimize any actions, even the most antisocial ones.)

3. The theory must identify ethical guidelines that would prohibit the unlimited pursuit of self-interest.

4. The theory must help us to solve ethical problems.

Some Traditional Assumptions of Ethical Theories

Before discussing specific ethical theories, it is important to understand some basic concepts. Many, but not all, ethical theories have centered on what might be called a set of "traditional ethical assumptions." Today some philosophers are calling into question these traditional ethical assumptions, but they remain important to many others. Traditional ethical assumptions provide a foundation for some ethical theories. These assumptions include:

1. Ethics is rational.
2. Persons are moral equals.
3. A person can universalize legitimate ethical evaluations.

Rationality

In the context of these traditional ethical assumptions, saying that ethics is rational means, in general, that we can use reason to reach theoretical and practical conclusions about ethical matters. More specifically, people can provide reasons to support moral guidelines and solutions to ethical problems; these reasons can be evaluated; and some guidelines and solutions are better than others. It also means that well-intentioned people who share an ethical framework (and sometimes even ones who do not) can discuss ethical problems and hope to arrive at mutually acceptable solutions.

Rationality is an important consideration related to ethics. It is a criterion for moral responsibility and is crucial to being a moral agent. *Moral agents* can be defined as beings who can perform morally significant actions and be held morally responsible for them. When we hold people morally responsible or accountable for something, we often feel justified in praising, rewarding, blaming, criticizing, or punishing them. There are three common criteria for moral responsibility. To be held morally responsible for something, an agent: (1) needs to have freely or willingly caused something to happen, or allowed it to happen through his or her negligence; (2) must be able to have known or must know the consequences of the thing; and (3) must be rational, or able to know the difference between good and evil.

The first criterion means that if my brakes fail and I try to avoid hitting other cars but accidentally run into yours, then I am not morally responsible for injuring you. You should not criticize me unless you believe that I could have done something to avoid the collision. My car struck yours, and I may be financially responsible for paying compensation. But I am not morally responsible because I did not freely or willingly hit your car. If, however, I have been negligent (for example, if I have been having a serious problem with my brakes but deliberately failed to get them fixed), then I am morally responsible for your injury.

The second criterion implies that I am not morally responsible if I cannot know the consequences of something, but I may be held morally responsible if I deliberately remain ignorant. If it were impossible for me to have known that my brakes would fail, I am not morally responsible for injuring you. If, however, I strongly suspected that there was a problem with my brakes, but deliberately chose to remain ignorant about their condition, then I will be held morally responsible for your injuries. I freely or willingly chose to remain ignorant of a potentially dangerous situation, and, therefore, we may say that the second criterion is satisfied.

The third criterion for moral responsibility means that insane or mentally defective people and young children who do not understand the difference between good and evil cannot be held morally responsible. For example, some insane people cannot understand the nature of their actions or rationally evaluate the consequences. People may also be unable to comprehend the difference between good and evil. A psychopath may not be able to understand the difference between killing an ant or a human being. We do not hold the psychopath morally responsible for his or her action, even though the person is causally responsible for doing the killing and will be confined to an institution. The psychopath does not really understand what he or she is doing and cannot meet the third criterion.

Moral Equals

The second of the traditional ethical assumptions is that persons are moral equals. By this, we mean that everyone in a sufficiently similar situation counts the same when we are trying to make ethical judgments or resolve moral problems. We ignore "irrelevant factors" or factors that would make us give special treatment to someone and not treat him or her as equal to everyone else. For example, it is usually thought to be irrelevant that a person is my friend. In ethical matters, I must be impartial and treat my friend as a moral equal to other persons. The same is true for me. I cannot privilege myself but must consider myself a moral equal to others. Treating persons as moral equals sometimes conflicts with pursuing self-interest. When I act on self-interest, I may proceed as

if I had more moral worth than other persons do. In an ethically significant matter, I must recognize that I am only one among equals. I must
do what is good or right, not just what is best for me.

Moral equality can be illustrated by briefly discussing act utilitarianism, which is one ethical theory (see Chapter 3). *Act utilitarians* claim
that ethical actions provide the greatest net benefit for the greatest number of persons affected. To be ethical, we must be impartial while acting
in accord with this rule. We cannot treat our families, our friends, or
ourselves in a special or privileged way. Rather, we must treat everyone
as moral equals and take them into consideration in the same way that
any other person would be taken into account. For an act utilitarian,
every person is the same when calculating the benefit and harm produced by an action. A benefit to your spouse or child is the same as a
benefit to a stranger. In some cases what maximizes benefit for the
greatest number of persons might also be in your self-interest, but that
would merely be a coincidence. In many other cases, following the act
utilitarian rule will conflict with your self-interest. For example, I may
want to spend my fifty dollars on more CDs for my collection, but the
ethical thing to do might be to donate the sum to an effective charity
(I already have hundreds of CDs, and giving the money to the charity
would save lives). Contributing the money to charity and saving the
lives produces more benefit for a larger number of people than buying
the CDs. According to utilitarians, in some cases I must sacrifice my self-
interest to be ethical.

Act utilitarianism and some other ethical theories claim that people
are moral equals. These theories can be called *egalitarian* ethical theories. They can be contrasted with *nonegalitarian* ethical theories, which
do not treat all people as moral equals. Three egalitarian theories are
discussed in this book: act utilitarianism, Kantian ethics, and the moral
rights ethical theory. Three nonegalitarian theories are also examined:
ethical relativism, virtue ethics, and the ethic of care.

Philosophers sometimes use the phrase "morally significant beings"
to identify members of the moral community or beings who ought to
receive ethical consideration. *Full-status morally significant beings* receive
the highest degree of moral consideration. There may also be *second-
class morally significant beings* who receive some moral consideration but
are not treated the same as those with full status. Some people believe
that certain animals, such as gorillas, chimpanzees, dogs, and cats,
should receive some moral consideration. For example, it may be wrong
to kill them even though the value of their lives does not equal that of
human lives. A great deal of debate centers about the criteria for being a
full-status morally significant being. For people who value nonhuman

animals highly, questions also arise about the criteria for second-class moral consideration.

Universalizability

The last of the traditional ethical assumptions is that persons can universalize legitimate moral evaluations; that is, they can extend their ethical evaluations to anyone else in a sufficiently similar situation. Universalizability is connected to the crucial idea of moral equality—I can universalize my legitimate ethical evaluations because I am a moral equal to everyone else. As I stated earlier, act utilitarians claim that ethical actions provide the greatest net benefit for the greatest number of people. Based on this principle, the ethical thing for me to do in the example of the CDs is to give the money to charity. If it is the ethical thing for me to do, I can claim that it is the moral thing for anyone to do in a sufficiently similar situation. If we are all moral equals, there is no relevant difference between us that would justify someone else acting differently.

For it to be ethical for someone to act differently in the same moral situation, that person would have to have a different moral standing than the rest of us. This cannot be the case, however, since we are moral equals. In moral matters, everyone in a situation with sufficiently similar morally significant factors ought to do the same thing because they are all moral equals. Thus, we can universalize our legitimate moral evaluations, or extend them to other people in similar situations.

These three traditional ethical assumptions lie behind most ethical theories and have had a great deal of influence on ethics. Among contemporary philosophers, these assumptions about rationality, equality, and universalizability have become controversial and are being called into question. In this book you will encounter both theories that endorse these traditional ethical assumptions and ones that do not.

Basic Themes Associated with Ethics

In addition to the traditional assumptions connected to ethical theories, four basic ethical themes can also be identified. These themes can be developed in a variety of ways. Here I will set them up as opposing views and present them in the form of questions.

1. Are some actions, beliefs, or values always either good or evil?

2. What makes something good or evil; is it the consequences that are produced or the reasoning that leads up to it?

3. Should we faithfully follow general rules of behavior, or should we separately evaluate each action and belief?

4. Should the group, community, or majority of persons be the focus of ethics, or should the focus be on the individual?

The first theme is represented by the question: Are some actions, beliefs or values always either good or evil? As we shall see in Chapter 2, *ethical relativists* reply "no," stating that whether an action is good or evil depends on whether a society approves or disapproves of it. People in different societies sometimes approve and disapprove of different things; therefore, no actions are always good or evil. In contrast, *ethical objectivists* answer the question with a "yes." According to them, some actions are always good or evil. For example, rape and murder are always evil. Objectivists appeal to objective or "factual" considerations to demonstrate evil. The fact that rape and murder harm victims or cause pain and death could be appealed to as objective reasons why they are evil. This conflict between relative and objective ethical positions and conclusions is an important one in ethics.

Another significant theme in ethics can be introduced by the question: What makes something good or evil; is it the consequences that are produced or the reasoning that leads up to it? Although it might seem that the correct answer is a combination of the two, philosophers have often chosen to focus primarily on one or the other aspect. *Ethical consequentialists* believe that the goodness of something is a result of the consequences that it produces. Ethical egoists focus on the consequences to the individual, whereas utilitarians demand the greatest beneficial consequences for the greatest number of people affected. For a utilitarian, sending a check to a charity is not good unless some benefit actually results from it. *Deontologists* deny that good is a result of the consequences. They think this introduces a distressing element of luck into ethics. From the consequentialist perspective, I might try to do something good, but if I am unlucky and no good consequences result from my effort, I have not succeeded in performing a good action. Deontologists focus on the reasoning that leads up to something. They assert that if the right kind of reasoning motivates me to send a check to charity, the action is good regardless of the consequences. Many philosophers focus on actions as the main subject of ethical evaluations. In the previous discussion, we might assume that they are working with the following model of action:

Reasoning → *Action* → *Consequences*

Deontologists believe we should look at the reasoning that precedes the action to determine whether it is good or evil. Consequentialists believe we should look at the consequences produced by the action. Action is often the focus of ethical evaluations, but morally significant beliefs, attitudes, commitments, policies, and so on can also provide a focus for evaluation. This dispute between the ethical consequentialists and the deontologists is another important debate in ethics.

A third theme relates to this question: Should we faithfully follow general rules of behavior, or should we separately evaluate each action and belief? People who believe that general rules should guide our behavior feel that there are rules that should have no exceptions; for example, it is wrong to kill innocent people, it is wrong to steal, it is wrong to break a promise. People who want to evaluate things separately believe that we must be open to the possibility that we can appropriately make an exception to even the best moral rule. They want to evaluate each action as independently as possible based on some criterion. The criterion may be similar to a rule, but if it is, then the criterion is the only rule that they will always endorse.

The German philosopher Immanuel Kant (1724–1804) believed that some rules could never be broken by an ethical person. For example, it is wrong to break your promises. Like Kant, *rule utilitarians* also believe in following general rules, although unlike Kant, they evaluate the rules by considering the general consequences of following them. If having people always follow a rule produces a greater net benefit than their not doing so, then the rule ought to be followed in all cases. In contrast to Kant and rule utilitarians, act utilitarians claim that we must evaluate each action as independently as possible using the general criterion that what is ethical is what promotes the greatest net benefit for the greatest number of morally significant beings affected. They have one basic rule or criterion, the utilitarian maxim that we ought to maximize net benefit, but they use this rule to evaluate distinct actions, decisions, beliefs, and so on separately. Breaking your promise may be the ethical thing to do in one case, whereas in another instance it may be unethical.

The fourth important theme relates to the proper focus of ethical attention and benefit: Should the group, community, or majority of persons be the focus of ethics, or should the focus be on the individual? Utilitarians believe that the focus of ethics should be the greatest net benefit for the greatest number of morally significant beings. In some cases, utilitarians would sacrifice the individual for the greater good of the group because the benefit to the larger number of people outweighs that of the individual. Other philosophers discuss ethics using the language of moral rights (see Chapter 5). Proponents of moral rights focus on the individual. They would never sacrifice the individual for the group, at least not without the individual's consent. Moral rights are often seen as legitimate claims to protection for the essential aspects of the individual, such as life, liberty, and property. The point of providing this protection is to prevent the group from forcing individuals to give up elements that are essential to living successful lives. This debate about the focus of ethical attention is another important conflict in ethics.

Each of the ethical theories discussed in this book takes a position in relation to these four themes, and those positions will be discussed in subsequent chapters. In light of this discussion, you will begin to recognize the particular tools, or guidelines, that may help you solve ethical problems you face in day-to-day living.

Conclusion

In this chapter I have provided a brief introduction to ethics, *the investigation into the conceptual and theoretical ethical resources for solving ethical problems and into the solutions to them.* A variety of ethical concepts were identified: moral responsibility, moral agents, morally significant beings, traditional ethical assumptions, and four ethical themes. Ethics is important because ethical problems present us with serious dilemmas and have serious consequences. All of us are confronted with ethical dilemmas in our daily lives. Ethical theories provide guidelines to help us solve those problems.

QUESTIONS FOR REVIEW

Here are some questions to help you review the main concepts in this chapter.

1. What is ethics?
2. What is the difference between theoretical ethics and applied ethics?
3. How does ethics differ from religion? Identify one reason we should keep religion and ethics separate.
4. How does ethics differ from law?
5. What is an ethical theory, and what is an ethical theory supposed to do? What three things typically are provided by an ethical theory?
6. What criteria will be used to evaluate ethical theories?

7. What are the three traditional ethical assumptions?

8. What are moral agents? What criteria do we use to determine moral responsibility?

9. What is the difference between egalitarian and nonegalitarian ethical theories?

10. What (or who) are morally significant beings?

11. What are the four basic themes associated with ethics?

12. What position is endorsed by ethical objectivists?

13. How do deontologists and consequentialists differ in regard to the question of what makes something good or evil?

NOTES

1. This definition of ethics is centered around solving ethical problems and seems appropriate for a book designed for applied ethics classes. A more general definition of ethics is: "inquiry about ways of life and rules of conduct." *The Encyclopedia of Philosophy,* Vol. 3 (New York: Macmillan, 1967).

2. In this book "ethical" and "moral" are used as synonyms.

3. In this book the term "morality" means a moral code or set of moral principles, rules, ideals, or guidelines usually grounded in a moral theory.

4. Mary Midgley, *Can't We Make Moral Judgments?* (New York: St. Martin's Press, 1991), p. 57.

Chapter 2

Ethical Relativism

When we study people around the world, we observe what appear to be different ethical guidelines and disparate solutions to ethical problems. In Ireland the prevailing view is that abortion is wrong, whereas in China women who already have one child are encouraged to have abortions. Some observers conclude that these differences are primarily related to the fact that people live in different societies. *Ethical relativism* is an approach to ethics connected to the ethical insight that *a legitimate set of ethical guidelines is related to an actual society or group.* Ethical relativism claims that the only legitimate ethical guidelines are those of actual societies or groups and that good and evil are connected to these actual ethical guidelines. Because legitimate ethical guidelines are always associated with an actual society or group, and because these actual societies and groups do not endorse exactly the same ethical guidelines, there is no legitimate universal set of ethical guidelines. Philosophers offer many different accounts of ethical relativism, but the discussion in this chapter builds directly on these ideas. In this chapter I will also show how problems develop with ethical relativism when we try to move beyond these initial ideas to a better understanding of the view.

Ethical Relativism and Ethical Subjectivism

It is important to distinguish ethical relativism from *ethical subjectivism.* Many philosophers have developed positions that are rightly or wrongly considered subjectivist, among them Friedrich Nietszche, Jean-Paul Sartre, A. J. Ayer, and Charles Stevenson. The idea at the heart of Charles Stevenson's version of ethical subjectivism is that good and evil (or, to be more precise, moral judgments or expressions) are related to the feelings or attitudes of specific individuals.[1] According to this view, there could be no objective good and evil. Stevenson's idea is that moral language has both emotive and prescriptive functions. First let's look at the emotive function. Moral language expresses positive and negative feelings, or what might be called feelings of approval and disapproval. The phrase "stealing is evil" expresses the person's disapproval of stealing. It is like saying, "stealing, boo!" "Giving to charity is good" expresses approval and is the same as "giving to charity, yea!" The idea is that ethical judgments express a particular individual's feelings of approval and disapproval. The second aspect of moral language is that it possesses a prescriptive function; that is, it prescribes certain actions or is used to influence people to act in certain ways. In relation to this aspect of moral language, when I say "stealing is evil," I am trying to keep you from stealing. When I say "giving to charity is good," I am encouraging you to give to charity. This brief summary is only a rough sketch of Stevenson's view, but it should be adequate to help us differentiate ethical subjectivism from ethical relativism.[2] Ethical relativists claim that legitimate ethical guidelines are those of actual societies and that good and evil are connected to these societal guidelines. Ethical subjectivists take a different view, stating that *legitimate ethical guidelines are connected to particular individuals and that good and evil are associated with something about these individuals.*

Before returning to ethical relativism, let's briefly consider whether Stevenson's view would be successful as an ethical theory based on the criteria from Chapter 1. First, can ethical subjectivism identify some ethical guidelines? If we believe that moral language has a prescriptive function, and if we are not too rigid or exclusive about what counts as "ethical guidelines," the answer is that ethical subjectivism can identify some moral guidelines. Moral expressions or judgments are attempts to influence people either to do or not to do various things, and these attempts could be viewed as ethical guidelines. According to ethical subjectivism, individuals produce the ethical guidelines, and the theory informs us about how to identify them.

Ethical subjectivism runs into problems with the second criterion: An ethical theory must be able to show that some ethical guidelines are better than others. If the feelings of approval and disapproval of particular individuals determine the ethical guidelines, then any moral guideline would be legitimate if it were related to a judgment that actually expressed a feeling or an attitude. The expression of any feeling is presumably legitimate; therefore, the expression of one feeling cannot be better than the expression of another. Ethical subjectivism cannot demonstrate that some moral guidelines are better than others.

The third criterion—an ethical theory must identify moral guidelines that would prohibit the unlimited pursuit of self-interest—is also a serious problem for ethical subjectivism. Any expression of feeling or moral guideline is legitimate, including those related to the unlimited pursuit of self-interest. If I have a good feeling about beating people and taking their money whenever I am short of cash, then that self-interested action is good even though it harms another person. Based on ethical subjectivism, people may make moral judgments or express feelings contrary to or in support of the unlimited pursuit of self-interest. Ethical subjectivism cannot guarantee that the ethical guidelines will prohibit the unlimited pursuit of self-interest.

The fourth criterion is that the ethical theory must help us solve ethical problems. If solving ethical problems simply means that we can arrive at personal solutions, then ethical subjectivism can help solve moral problems. My feelings can guide me in solving ethical problems. If I experience a good feeling about stealing a book, then I should do it. If solving ethical problems includes being able to support my solutions with reasons that other people would understand and might even endorse, then ethical subjectivism cannot help us solve moral problems in a satisfactory way. My only reason for saying that stealing the book was good was that I had a good feeling about doing it. Presumably, I will not be able to explain why I have that good feeling. However, even if I could speculate about this, it is the feelings that are important to Stevenson, not the reasons why I have them.

Ethical subjectivism makes similar solutions to ethical problems mysterious. For example, if all the citizens in a society believe that abortion is evil, this could be only a coincidence, according to an ethical subjectivist. By coincidence, every individual would experience the same feeling of disapproval about abortion, and therefore all of them would say it is evil. In contrast, ethical relativists would say that we should expect the members of a given society to endorse the same moral guidelines and to make similar ethical judgments because these guidelines are created by the group.

Based on the serious problems with at least two of the four criteria, ethical subjectivism would not be a successful ethical theory. It would not help us live together successfully. Now let's turn our attention to the theory of ethical relativism.

One Version of Ethical Relativism

Ethical relativism relates good and evil to the ethical guidelines of actual societies or groups. It often starts from the observation that ethical beliefs and practices are not identical in all societies. This observation is at the heart of cultural relativism. *Cultural relativism* is the view that some societies have different sets of ethical guidelines. If individuals from these different societies were to discuss their ethical principles and practices, they would probably disagree about what practices were right and wrong. These ethical disagreements would arise even though the individuals agreed on the description of the practices (e.g., they agreed on what constituted an abortion).[3] The progression from cultural relativism to ethical relativism occurs when the observation about ethical differences is followed by the claim that a society's approval and disapproval create ethical guidelines and that these moral guidelines produce good and evil. If society approves of something, it is ethical, and if society disapproves of something, it is unethical. *The approval and disapproval of a particular society act as the ultimate ethical standard for determining good and evil.*

Ethical relativists maintain that there is no universal or objective ethical standard that holds for all societies at all times.[4] This idea is an essential claim of ethical relativism. Legitimate notions of good and evil often vary from society to society and may change within a society over time. Therefore, ethical guidelines are relative to some society or group in a particular historical setting. Different ethical positions may be appropriate for different peoples. No single legitimate set of ethical guidelines is endorsed by every society; therefore, no legitimate universal ethical guidelines can be identified.

Ethical Relativism and Tolerance

Based on these ideas, many people believe that ethical relativists ought to endorse tolerance for the different ethical guidelines and practices of other societies. They conclude that it is wrong for people in one society to condemn the moral guidelines or ethically significant practices of another. Without a legitimate set of universal ethical guidelines, condemnation by members of one society of the practices of another is unjustified. The ethical guidelines of one society would have no legitimate application to any other society.

This idea is usually illustrated with an example about some ethically significant practice that is simultaneously endorsed by one society and condemned by another. For instance, modern-day Cuba presumably still condemns capitalism as exploitative and evil. In contrast, the ethical guidelines of the United States endorse capitalism. Here it seems that both of these societies would agree on a description of capitalism. The ethical relativist would suggest that the different moral guidelines produced different moral evaluations of capitalism. Capitalism is ethically right for citizens of the United States and ethically wrong for Cubans. Neither group is objectively right or wrong; therefore, each group should tolerate rather than condemn the other.

I believe it is a mistake to include in ethical relativism the idea of tolerance for the different ethical guidelines and ethically significant practices of other societies. This position supporting cross-cultural tolerance is a serious problem for ethical relativism, and the theory will operate without it. Bernard Williams, a contemporary British philosopher, explains that the assertion that we should not condemn the different beliefs and practices of other societies is a nonrelative or objective claim, and the ethical relativist has no grounding for such a claim.

> The central confusion of relativism is to try to conjure out of the fact that societies have differing attitudes and values an a priori nonrelative principle to determine the attitude of one society toward another; this is impossible.[5]

It is an impossibility because, according to ethical relativism, people have no basis for making ethical claims that are not related to the actual moral guidelines of their society.

The most that ethical relativists are justified in claiming is that in our society we approve of tolerance or noninterference with other cultures and hence we should be tolerant. This, however, is not the position endorsed by the proponents of cross-cultural tolerance. They assert that everyone ought to tolerate the ethical differences of other societies regardless of their own moral guidelines. Williams's point is that there is no justification for this claim about what everyone should do. In the United States, we seem to approve of interference with other cultures and societies. We intervene regularly in the interest of promoting peace and preventing violations of moral rights. Ethical relativists have no grounds for condemning our interference if such intervention is approved by our society.

This idea, that we should leave cross-cultural tolerance out of ethical relativism, can be illustrated with an example. Assume that moral rights are part of the ethical guidelines endorsed by American society. Rose is an ethical relativist and therefore believes that the legitimate moral guidelines are those approved of by her society. She is especially insistent about the right to life. When she sees people in other countries being killed merely because of their political views or because they belong to certain ethnic groups, she claims the killing is evil and ought to be stopped. Rose's view of good and evil is based on the moral guidelines of her society—the only legitimate ethical standard available to her—and in her view other societies are acting unethically when they execute people for political reasons. Rose is not tolerant of these executions; she condemns them (and perhaps wants to eliminate them). She would not tolerate a society like Nazi Germany but rather would condemn it and want to see it destroyed.

To avoid Williams's problem, ethical relativism should endorse the idea that people will use the moral guidelines of their own society to evaluate everything. The key to ethical relativism is that good and evil are established by the actual moral guidelines of a society, and those actual guidelines may not include cross-cultural tolerance. Only if a society's actual moral guidelines include the principle of tolerance should citizens of that society tolerate the different ethical guidelines and practices of other societies. Although this version of ethical relativism avoids the serious problem with cross-cultural tolerance, it will have other problems. Before discussing them, however, I want to provide some support for the theory and discuss how it relates to the ethical assumptions and themes.

Justification and Determining the Morally Significant

One of the things we look for in an ethical theory is a justification for the ethical standard. Why would someone endorse the ethical standard put forward by ethical relativism? There would seem to be two main arguments. The first is based on cultural relativism. A simple version of it goes like this. We observe that ethical guidelines vary from society to society (or are relative to a society). Therefore, ethical guidelines ought to vary from society to society, and no single set of guidelines is correct for all societies. If no single set is correct for all societies, then something about each particular society (approval and disapproval) must create legitimate ethical guidelines. This argument is, of course, incorrect. Just because things are a certain way does not allow us to conclude that they ought to be that way. The fact that there are many children starving in the world today does not necessitate the conclusion that they ought to be starving. If you think that they ought to be starving, you need a separate argument to try to support that conclusion. From the observation that ethical guidelines vary from society to society, there can be no justified conclusion about what the correct ethical guidelines ought to be. Perhaps ethical guidelines ought to vary from society to society, and perhaps no one set of guidelines is correct for all societies. However, it is also possible that there is one correct set of ethical guidelines and that the people in many societies are simply wrong. Cultural relativism does not provide adequate support for ethical relativism.

A second and better reason for endorsing ethical relativism is similar to one of the tasks of an ethical theory. People might endorse the theory because they view morality, or a set of ethical guidelines, as a social institution. Societies create various institutions to help them function successfully. One such institution is morality. Morality is necessary because the laws, by themselves, are not adequate to produce the kinds of behavior that will allow society to operate successfully. (This idea was discussed in Chapter 1.) People need to respect other people's lives, liberty, property, and privacy to produce a successfully functioning society. Without morality, people will only respect these things when they believe they might get caught and punished. Morality helps society function more successfully, and the best way to create a morality is to ground it in social approval and disapproval. This reasoning acts as the justification for using the ethical standard of social approval and disapproval and for basing good and evil on the actual ethical guidelines of a society.

Each society creates the morality or set of moral guidelines that will best help the society function well. Cubans presumably disapprove of capitalism because they think it will harm their society and individuals in it. They claim that capitalism produces class conflict and other problems. Americans, in contrast, believe that capitalism is the only system that can create an efficient economy. Capitalism is necessary for our society to operate successfully. Adopting this justification for ethical relativism supports the idea that each society has a legitimate set of moral guidelines and that good and evil are related to them.

The third thing we look for in an ethical theory is a delineation between what is and is not morally significant. This is not an issue that ethical relativists frequently discuss, but according to one plausible view, moral relativists believe that if society disapproves or approves of something it is morally significant. Of course, the stronger the approval or disapproval, the more morally significant the thing is. Most societies approve of keeping promises and disapprove of breaking them; therefore, keeping promises is morally significant in these societies. If society does not approve or disapprove of something, it is not morally significant. For example, society has no opinion about whether you should put your right or left sock on first; therefore this action has no moral significance.

Ethical Relativism and the Traditional Ethical Assumptions

Ethical relativism agrees with two of the traditional ethical assumptions but rejects the other one. Ethical relativists would agree that ethics is rational. People can provide reasons to support their ethical guidelines and their solutions to moral problems. The merits of these reasons can be discussed, and solutions can be evaluated. For ethical relativists, the most compelling reason to accept a solution would probably be that the majority of people in the society approve of it. Ethical relativists would also agree that well-intentioned people who share a set of actual ethical guidelines could discuss moral problems and arrive at mutually acceptable solutions. Two ethical relativists who are Chinese citizens should agree that if a particular woman is pregnant with her second child, the ethical thing to do is to have an abortion.

Whether or not ethical relativism accepts moral equality is an interesting question. In one sense it does: all members of a particular society are moral equals in the sense that the moral guidelines of their society bind all of them. Also, all people are moral equals in the sense that I judge all of them by the same set of moral guidelines, those of my society. In a wider sense, however, all human beings are not moral equals; members of another society are not treated in the same way as members of a person's own society. The actions of members of other societies are not judged by the moral guidelines of their own societies but by the moral guidelines of the society of the person doing the judging. For example, I judge myself and the members of my society by the moral guidelines of the United States, which are our guidelines, but I also judge members of other societies by the moral guidelines of the United States, which are foreign to them. Therefore, ethical relativists judge some people by ethical guidelines that those people accept and other people by ethical guidelines that are foreign to them and that they would probably not accept. On the whole, this version of ethical relativism does not consider people to be moral equals because it does not judge all people by their own society's ethical guidelines.

The version of ethical relativism that I elaborated could accept the idea that people are capable of universalizing legitimate moral evaluations. If we simply apply the ethical guidelines of our own society to everyone, then we are universalizing our moral evaluations. The version of ethical relativism that includes cross-cultural tolerance would not universalize moral evaluations. The appropriate ethical evaluations of the members of other societies should be based on their own ethical guidelines. These guidelines might be the same as ours, and we might reach the same ethical conclusion. However, that conclusion would be grounded in the particular ethical guidelines of each society; it would not come about by universalizing our guidelines.

Ethical Relativism and the Four Basic Ethical Themes

Ethical relativism takes a position on each of the ethical themes discussed in Chapter 1. The first theme was represented by this question: Are some actions, beliefs, or values always either good or evil? Ethical relativists answer this question with a "no." Legitimate ethical guidelines are those endorsed by an actual society, and such guidelines may change. For example, at one time slavery was ethical in the United States because it was endorsed by the society's ethical guidelines. Today slavery is unethical because the moral guidelines of the United States disapprove of it. The same thing could potentially happen to any action, belief, or value.

The second ethical theme was highlighted by this question: What makes something good or evil; is it the consequences that are produced or the reasoning that leads up to it? Ethical relativists seem to believe that it is the reasoning that leads up to something that makes it ethical. If an action is approved by a society's moral guidelines, then that action is ethical regardless of the consequences. The ethical guidelines of the society create good and evil. Even though society may refer to consequences in creating those guidelines, what is of primary importance for ethical relativism is whether or not the action is in accord with the society's guidelines.

A third ethical theme relates to this question: Should we faithfully follow general rules of behavior, or should we separately evaluate each action and belief? The position of ethical relativism in relation to this theme is debatable, but I believe ethical relativists would be compelled to claim that we should faithfully follow the moral rules of our society. If society believes that stealing other people's property is evil, then stealing is always evil, no matter what the benefit to the individual. Allowing exceptions to the basic moral rules of society would violate the idea that society needs morality to function smoothly. Of course, if the belief is that sometimes it is ethical to steal and other times it is not, then people would still be following a general rule even if they steal on some occasions and not on others.

The fourth important ethical theme relates to the proper focus of ethical attention. Should the group, community, or majority of persons be the focus of ethics, or should the focus be on the individual? Ethical relativists focus on the group or society as the source of legitimate ethical guidelines. Individuals who disagree with the moral guidelines of their society and hold different ones will not be acting ethically if they act in accord with their personal moral principles and in opposition to the societal ethical principles. It is the actual ethical guidelines of the society or the group that are identified as the legitimate moral guidelines by ethical relativism.

Problems with Ethical Relativism

Until now I have presented and briefly elaborated on the ethical insight central to ethical relativism: that a legitimate set of ethical guidelines is related to an actual society, culture, or group. In this section, you will see that problems develop with the theory as we try to fill out the basic ideas of ethical relativism and develop a better understanding of the theory. As I discuss the problems, I will try to relate them to the criteria for evaluating ethical theories that were presented in Chapter 1.

Actual Ethical Guidelines

The first step to a better understanding of ethical relativism is to try to locate the actual ethical guidelines of a society. This will help us to better understand what the ethical relativist means by the ethical guidelines of a society. Assume that I am an ethical relativist and a citizen of the United States; I must know the ethical guidelines of my country so that I can follow them. I am, of course, assuming that the society as a whole has a set of ethical guidelines.

Where do I find the actual ethical guidelines of my society? Laws are written down and can be discovered in law libraries, but ethical guidelines are not recorded in ethics libraries. There is no determinate set of ethical guidelines written down for the guidance of American citizens. If there is an unwritten set, I am not aware of them. Therefore, I will have to look for them. There would seem to be four promising alternatives.

One way to find the actual ethical guidelines of a society would be to examine the beliefs of the majority of the members of the society. To discover what guidelines were actually endorsed—for example, if I wanted to know whether my society approved of abortion—I might take a survey. In doing this I would be assuming that other people are more knowledgeable than I am—even though I am a concerned citizen (and a teacher of ethics). I am hoping that they know the ethical guidelines of our society and will respond to the survey based on them. They have to respond to the survey based on the ethical guidelines of our society and not on their personal preferences or feelings. If they did the latter, the results would reflect an ethical subjectivist approach. The ethical relativist position is not supposed to be that the ethical guidelines of society are simply the subjective guidelines of the majority of the citizens. This would result in the foundation of the social ethical guidelines (the citizens' subjective beliefs) being plagued with all the problems of ethical subjectivism, a set of problems that led me to conclude that ethical subjectivism would be unsuccessful as an ethical theory. Ethical guidelines are legitimate because society approves of them. However, if we do not already know what society approves of or what the ethical guidelines really are, this method will not be a successful way of discovering them. For example, there would be no way to know how to respond to the survey question about abortion unless we already knew whether or not our society approves of it. I do not believe that citizens know what society approves and disapproves in all cases; therefore, this approach would be unsatisfactory. If we are unclear about the ethical guidelines, we could not discover them using this method.

Another idea would be to look at the guidelines of the government or ruling group. Perhaps the government should establish the ethical guidelines for the society. We would have to discover if the government approved of abortion. Of course, this would be odd in the United States since the president and members of Congress try to reflect the opinions of their constituents. This method would not seem to work in the United States unless the first method worked, and I have argued that it is unsuccessful. In a dictatorship we could discover the ethical guidelines if they were grounded in the feelings of the dictator and he or she imposed them on the whole society. We would need to know whether the dictator had a good feeling about abortion. The problem with this variation is that the social ethical guidelines are founded on the dictator's feelings, and once again the foundation of the social moral guidelines would have the problems that affect ethical subjectivism. Therefore, this second approach to discovering the actual ethical guidelines is unsuccessful also.

A third possibility would be to examine the laws and then work backward. The assumption would be that ethical guidelines inspire laws. By looking at the law, we could attempt to discover the society's moral guidelines. The law allows abortion, so abortion must have been ethical when the law was made. This view implies that although we are unclear about the ethical guidelines of today people in the past must have been better informed. They were clear enough about the ethical guidelines to make laws based on them. The problem is that the ethical guidelines are supposed to be based on what is approved and disapproved of by society, but this "legal view" takes the approval and disapproval away from the current society and gives the authority to establish ethical guidelines to the earlier version of society that created the laws. This seems illegitimate for ethical relativism. These ethical guidelines are for an earlier version of society, and we would not know if they are still the ethical guidelines of our society.

A fourth possibility would be to look at the society's moral tradition. Presumably this moral tradition would be articulated in the society's fundamental documents. These would not have to be merely political documents; they might also include works of literature, art, and so on. We would have to discover whether or not the moral tradition of the United States approved of abortion. As ethical relativists, however, why should we be bound by moral tradition? Moral guidelines are based on what is approved and disapproved of by society. Moral tradition takes the approval and disapproval away from our current society and places the authority to establish ethical guidelines on some earlier version of our society. Once again, this seems incorrect because we would not know if these are still the ethical guidelines of our society.

All of these are possibilities for discovering the actual ethical beliefs of a society. One could also conceivably assert that the correct morality would be the intersection of all of them. In any case, the difficulty is obvious and twofold: (1) all of the ways of identifying the actual ethical guidelines are seriously problematic, and (2) we have no way to choose among them. In general, the problem for ethical relativism is that the theory does not seem to be able to identify the actual moral guidelines of a society. This implies that ethical relativism cannot satisfy any of the criteria for evaluating ethical theories. The first criterion states that the ethical theory must be able to identify some ethical guidelines. If we cannot determine the actual moral guidelines of our society, then the idea proposed by ethical relativism about how to identify the ethical guidelines is incorrect. Ethical relativism will not be able to identify the necessary moral guidelines, nor can it satisfy any of the other criteria. It is not successful as an ethical theory.

Multiple Sets of Ethical Guidelines

A better understanding of ethical relativism also requires us to determine whether the ethical guidelines of other groups, besides society as a whole, should count as legitimate moral guidelines. If the ethical guidelines endorsed by ethnic groups, local communities, special interest groups, and so on count, ethical relativism will have to deal with multiple sets of legitimate moral guidelines that may conflict. For the sake of this discussion, we shall assume that these groups have ethical guidelines that are written down. (If they do not, the first problem would apply to them as well as to society as a whole.) Imagine that Rose is a citizen of the United States, but she is also a member of other groups with their own particular ethical beliefs. She is a woman, Hispanic, part of a family, and a resident of a local community. She also works for a large corporation. If all of these groups have ethical guidelines, would each set constitute legitimate guidelines? If they are all legitimate ethical guidelines, how should she resolve conflicts among them? Suppose the majority of women in the United States are "pro-choice," the majority of Hispanics "pro-life," the majority of her family "pro-life," the majority of people in her local community "pro-choice," and the position of her corporation is "pro-choice." As an ethical relativist, Rose cannot determine which position to take on abortion. This situation would seem to imply that ethical relativism has additional problems with at least the second and fourth criteria for evaluating the ethical theories. In connection with the second one, ethical relativism would not be able to demonstrate that one set of moral guidelines is better than another. The fourth criterion states that the theory must help us solve ethical problems, but if Rose was faced with the problem of whether or not to get an abortion, ethical relativism would be unable to help her resolve the dilemma.

Some form of ethical relativism (usually the kind involving cross-cultural tolerance) seems more plausible if we concentrate on tribes that are isolated in remote regions or on islands. It is relatively easy to regard a tribe on an isolated island as a distinct group or community. In the pluralistic contemporary world, however, it is much harder to find such distinctive societies. We tend to belong to a number of groups (an ethnic group, a socioeconomic class, a country, a company, a local community, a family, and so on). Given the existence of multiple groups with legitimate ethical guidelines, ethical relativism will not be a successful ethical theory because it will neither identify unambiguous ethical guidelines nor show why some moral guidelines are better than others.

This problem with multiple groups could be solved if we interpret the ethical relativist as saying that only the moral guidelines of the society as a whole count as legitimate ethical guidelines. This solution, however, makes resolving the first problem even more crucial, and we could not solve it.

Moral Progress and Dissent

An ethical theory must be able to identify some moral guidelines, but ethical relativism makes the production and identification of new ethical guidelines mysterious. Legitimate ethical guidelines are those that are approved of by the society, and we know that sometimes these change (e.g., slavery is now unethical in the United States). The mystery is that guidelines change when there is no apparent reason why they would. Good and evil depend on the approval and disapproval of a society, not on objective reasons why the society approves or disapproves, such as that people are being benefited or harmed. (If we grounded moral guidelines on objective reasons, we would have another ethical theory, perhaps act utilitarianism.) If, however, the reasons why we approve and disapprove of things are not important, then there is no motivation for change in the ethical guidelines. Without any motivation for change, it is a mystery why a society would do so.

Another aspect of the mysterious nature of the production and identification of new ethical guidelines surfaces when we think about what ethical relativists must say about the relation between the moral guidelines of a society and the people who disagree with those guidelines. For them, there can be no legitimate ethical dissent within a society. If "good" equates to whatever is approved of by the society, then members of the society who dissent from the dominant ethical guidelines would always be wrong. In pre–Civil War Alabama, a member of the white community who believed that slavery was evil would be wrong. According to an ethical relativist, good and evil for whites was determined by the white community at large or by the prevailing view in Southern society, not by dissenters. The slaves might agree with the dissenter, but since the dissenter is not a member of the slave community, the ethical position of that community cannot legitimate his or her dissent. The problem here is that dissent is always wrong, but dissent is a major factor in changing a society's ethical beliefs. Once again the production of new ethical guidelines seems mysterious.

Conclusion

Although grounded in a reasonable ethical insight, ethical relativism is not a successful ethical theory based on the criteria established in Chapter 1. Although many moral beliefs are held by individual members of a society, we cannot identify the actual ethical guidelines of the society as a whole. Therefore, ethical relativism does not meet any of the criteria for a successful ethical theory. In the next chapter we will look at act utilitarianism, an ethical theory that does a better job of solving ethical problems and helping us to live together successfully.

QUESTIONS FOR REVIEW

Here are some questions to help you review the main concepts in this chapter.

1. What ethical insight is related to ethical relativism?
2. What is ethical subjectivism? Could ethical subjectivism be successful as an ethical theory? Support your answer.
3. What observation do ethical relativists make about societies?
4. What standard do ethical relativists use to determine good and evil?
5. Why shouldn't ethical relativism include cross-cultural tolerance?
6. What is the best justification for ethical relativism?
7. How do ethical relativists differentiate between what is and what is not morally significant?

8. What would ethical relativists say about each of the three aspects of the traditional ethical assumptions?

9. What position does ethical relativism take on each of the four ethical themes?

10. Which problem with ethical relativism is the most serious? Explain why.

11. Is ethical relativism a successful ethical theory? Support your answer.

NOTES

1. Charles L. Stevenson, *Ethics and Language* (New Haven: Yale University Press, 1944).

2. In my opinion moral language does not work as Stevenson thought it did. It is beyond the scope of this book, however, to analyze the meaning of various ethical expressions.

3. This assumes that people from different societies could agree on the descriptions of the practices (e.g., what counts as a lie, a bribe, a theft, or self-defense). A more radical version of ethical relativism claims that people from different societies could not even agree on the descriptions of the practices.

4. There could be a legitimate universal moral code if by coincidence all societies developed the same set of moral guidelines. This, of course, has not happened so far.

5. Bernard Williams, *Morality: An Introduction to Ethics* (New York: Harper & Row, 1972), p. 23.

Chapter 3

Act Utilitarianism

In Chapter 2 we saw the difficulty in identifying the actual ethical guidelines of a society. Yet without such guidelines, how do we make ethical judgments? Every day people do things we easily classify as good or evil. When I read in the newspaper that a woman has been violently raped and murdered, I do not have to consult the ethical guidelines of my society to conclude that the act is evil. The woman has been harmed and killed, and that is sufficient for me.

Act utilitarianism can explain how I reached my conclusion. It is an ethical theory that focuses on harm and benefit to morally significant beings. Act utilitarianism is related to the ethical insight that *an action is morally bad if it harms someone, whereas it is morally good if it helps or benefits someone.* Many people think about good and evil in this way. When you consider whether or not to do something that will affect others, do you think about whether anyone will be harmed or helped by your action? If you do, then act utilitarianism may appeal to you.

When we focus on the harm and benefit produced by our actions, we are looking at the results or consequences of those actions. Ethical theories that claim that good and evil are related to consequences or results are called *consequentialist ethical theories.* Act utilitarianism is a consequentialist ethical theory that provides a means to evaluate particular actions.

Act Utilitarianism and Ethical Egoism

Another consequentialist ethical theory is called *ethical egoism.* This theory might also follow from the previous insight, and hence it is important to briefly explain one version of it so that we can differentiate it from act utilitarianism. Ethical egoism claims that to act ethically moral agents should act in their own self-interest and maximize benefit for themselves. In other words, what is good is what produces a net benefit for a particular individual. Ethical egoism leads to the conclusion that there is no difference between "good for me" and "good." If it is beneficial for me to assault you and steal your money because I need it, and if I know I can do it without being caught, and I will not be bothered by bad feelings about it afterwards, then it is good to do it.

This version of ethical egoism is making a claim about how everyone should act: everyone should act based on his or her own self-interest. You will act to maximize benefit to you, and I will act to maximize benefit to me. This ethical position does not mean that a person can never act in a way that would benefit someone else. If helping someone else is the best way to maximize benefit to me, then I should help that person. If I depend on another person for a ride to work each day, it would be consistent with ethical egoism for me to lend that person a hundred dollars to get the car fixed. Although I am temporarily out the hundred dollars, I gain the significant benefit of being able to go to work and make money. Ethical egoism does not claim that I should always do what is pleasant. I should be rational about what is best for me. I regard exercising for an hour every day as unpleasant, but as an ethical egoist, I should probably do it because it would produce significant benefits for me.

This short summary of one version of ethical egoism is sufficient to allow us to differentiate it from act utilitarianism. Before doing so, however, I will consider whether ethical egoism would be a successful ethical theory based on the criteria in Chapter 1. First, can ethical egoism identify some ethical guidelines? The theory does identify a basic ethical guideline: people should act based on their own self-interest and maximize net benefit to themselves. We can use this guideline to evaluate particular cases. For example, in this situation I should lie because it will produce more benefit than harm for me. Second, the theory can also show that some ethical guidelines are better than others. "I should lie in this situation" is a better guideline than "I should tell the truth" because the first one will maximize net benefit to me. To skip to the fourth criterion, ethical egoism can help us to solve moral problems using these guidelines. However, the theory does not satisfy the third criterion. Nothing in the guidelines identified by the theory prohibits the unlimited pursuit of self-interest. The ethical guidelines would imply that you ought to pursue self-interest in any and all ways that maximize benefit to you. It would permit antisocial acts that are harmful to others or to society in general if these acts benefit the individual ethical egoist. Therefore, ethical egoism is not a successful ethical theory based on the criteria from Chapter 1. It does not identify ethical guidelines that would control the unlimited pursuit of self-interest and help us to live together successfully.

Ethical egoism and act utilitarianism are both consequentialist ethical theories, yet there is an important difference between them. Ethical egoism states that moral agents should act in their own self-interest and maximize net benefit for themselves. In other words, what is good is what produces a net benefit for a particular individual. In contrast, act utilitarianism claims that moral agents should maximize net benefit for the greatest number of morally significant beings affected by a certain action. As a utilitarian, I cannot merely act in my own self-interest; I must consider everyone who will be benefited or harmed. The utilitarian position and the difference between it and ethical egoism will become even clearer in the remainder of this chapter.

The Essential Principle and Standard of Act Utilitarianism

Act utilitarianism was popularized by two British thinkers, Jeremy Bentham (1748–1832) and John Stuart Mill (1806–1873). They centered their ideas on a common principle: *What is good is what promotes the greatest net utility for the greatest number of sentient beings (beings capable of having sensations).* "Utility" roughly means usefulness, but both Bentham and Mill understood utility in terms of another concept. Bentham claimed that what was good was what promoted the greatest net *pleasure* for the greatest number of sentient beings. Mill argued that what was good was what promoted the greatest net *happiness* for the greatest number of sentient beings. These two formulations are similar in one sense; both Bentham and Mill thought that pleasure was the essential component of happiness. They differ in that Bentham focused on pleasure and pain, whereas Mill attempted to broaden that focus. Another important difference was that Mill added the idea that there were different *qualities* of pleasure or happiness. For example, intellectual or spiritual pleasures were better than purely physical ones.

For the purpose of this book, I will replace "utility" with a third concept. My version of the utilitarian principle and the ethical standard for determining good and evil is: *What is good is what promotes the greatest net benefit for the greatest number of morally significant beings affected; what is bad is what promotes the greatest net harm for the greatest number of morally significant beings affected.* I favor this formulation of the utilitarian rule because the terms "pleasure" and "happiness" can lead people astray. In the ordinary sense of "pleasure" and "happiness," some things may not be pleasant or make us happy, but they may still be good. Learning is not always pleasant, nor does it always produce happiness, especially when we have to work very hard to acquire the knowledge. Learning, however, is often beneficial or good even if it is not pleasant. Another consideration is that some people reject the idea that pleasure is good. People sometimes pursue pleasure early in life, but then tire of it. They may then seek success, fame, or power. They may choose to serve others or to serve God in a life of self-sacrifice. They may seek knowledge or enlightenment. Ultimately, they follow the path that seems most beneficial. A key idea for act utilitarianism is that it is good to do things that make morally significant beings better off and bad to do things that harm them. In my opinion, "benefit" and "harm" articulate this utilitarian idea better than "pleasure" and "happiness."

Benefit and Harm

Although I think "benefit" and "harm" lead to fewer misunderstandings, the idea of using these terms with utilitarianism does have some problems. Many philosophers believe that we should not use philosophical terms unless we can define them in a very precise way. One way of doing this is to provide the necessary and sufficient conditions, attributes, or characteristics of the thing being defined. By necessary characteristics, philosophers mean those characteristics that must be possessed by the members of a class; for example, having three sides is a necessary characteristic of the class of triangles. The sufficient characteristics are all the characteristics that guarantee that something is a member of a class. The sufficient attributes of triangles would guarantee when a polygon is a triangle. This set of attributes would work—two dimensional, three-sided, rectilinear, closed, figure where the sum of the interior angles equals 180 degrees—although perhaps a smaller set would also be sufficient to differentiate triangles from other polygons. These kinds of definitions may be found or perhaps created for concepts important to mathematics or science, such as "triangle" and "igneous rock," but I do not believe this kind of definition is possible for ethical terms.

In ethics, we must get by with vague definitions and then work out the application of these concepts by using definitions, paradigm cases, and common sense. To benefit someone is to make him or her better off; to improve the person's condition; to help him or her to flourish; to make someone healthier, wiser, happier, more ethical, and so on. This is a rather vague definition and contains many concepts that are difficult and controversial. What exactly is "better off"? How can we know if something "improves a person's condition"? What is the meaning of "flourish"? In many cases we will have to work out whether an action is beneficial or not. Does spanking a child when he or she does something wrong benefit the child? This could be a very difficult question to answer, but the problem is not a failure to understand "benefit." The difficulty is that we are not certain whether spanking the child actually does make the child better off. Does spanking produce the benefit of improved behavior? Is the pain and humiliation produced by spanking outweighed by the improved behavior? Is the child more likely to flourish after being spanked? Philosophers are not the best people to answer these questions. We would need to consult experts in the growth, development, and psychology of children to try to find the answers. By consulting the relevant experts, it is possible that we could find answers to these questions and resolve the ethical issue connected to spanking. Thus, I will claim that even though we must rely on vague definitions for "harm" and "benefit," it is still possible to use these terms as essential components of act utilitarianism.

Justification and Determining the Morally Significant

One way to provide a justification for using this particular ethical standard is to claim that benefit is the ultimate end of all our activities, and that we should use whatever is the ultimate end of all our activities as our standard of ethical evaluation. Some of our goals have *instrumental value* because they are a means to achieve other goals. I may want to get a good grade on a test so that I can earn a good grade in a course. The good grade on the test is a *means* to achieve the *end* of the good grade in the course. The good grade in the course is a means to a further end—graduating from college with a good grade point average. Graduating from college with a good grade point average may be a means to the end of getting a good job, and getting a good job may be the means to obtain money. The money allows me to buy a house, a car, and other possessions. It allows me to take vacations and so on. Why do I want these possessions and vacations? They are the means to happiness, but why do I want to be happy? I believe that I am better off when I am happy than when I am unhappy. In other words, happiness is beneficial. The whole chain ultimately ends with what is beneficial to us. Philosophers would say that whatever lies at the end of the chain possesses *intrinsic value.* The utilitarian justification is that benefit has intrinsic value and that we should use whatever has intrinsic value to ethically evaluate our actions and beliefs.

The standard endorsed by act utilitarians provides a means of separating the morally significant from what is not morally significant. Whatever produces a significant benefit or harm for a morally significant being and is brought about by a moral agent is morally significant. Matters that have no significant benefit or harm are not morally significant (e.g., whether you put on your left or right sock first).

Amendments to the Original Insight

The original insight that benefiting persons is good and harming them is bad must be amended to be congruent with act utilitarianism. If helping one morally significant being is good, helping several is even better. In a similar way, the more morally significant beings we harm, the worse the action is. This idea that what is good is what benefits the *greatest number* of morally significant beings involved is essential to act utilitarianism.

I have used the term "morally significant beings" to identify those beings whose benefit and harm we must take into consideration to act ethically (see Chapter 1). Who are morally significant beings? A practical version of act utilitarianism requires a criterion or set of criteria that identifies those beings whose harm and benefit must be considered. Bentham thought that any being who could experience pain and pleasure must be considered. This would presumably include all mammals because they have nervous systems like ours and probably experience pain and pleasure. Peter Singer, a contemporary act utilitarian, claims that the capacity to have interests is the crucial criterion, although he adds that, "The capacity for suffering and enjoying things is a prerequisite for having interests at all, a condition that must be satisfied before we can speak of interests in any meaningful way."[1] Singer adds that sentience is enough to make a being worthy of equal consideration of interests, so his position may not be very different from Bentham's.[2] Singer would also presumably include all mammals as morally significant beings, although he says that a stronger case can be made for some of them such as chimpanzees, gorillas, and orangutans. In contrast to Bentham, moral philosophers working on topics like abortion have suggested more demanding criteria for full moral significance. In "On the Moral and Legal Status of Abortion," Mary Anne Warren suggests five traits that are central to full moral consideration: consciousness, reasoning, self-motivated activity, the capacity to communicate, and the presence of a self-concept and self-awareness.[3] If we used these criteria to determine whose harm and benefit must be considered, most mammals would not qualify. Act utilitarianism will work with any set of criteria, as long as they are clear. The crucial point is that act utilitarianism does not necessarily limit to human beings the set of beings whose harm and benefit we must consider.

Another supplement to the basic insight is that some benefits are more significant than others. If I pay for your college education, it is a more significant benefit than buying you a glass of milk, although both are usually beneficial. It is, of course, the same with harms; some are more significant than others. Therefore, act utilitarians look at the significance of the harms and benefits and the number of morally significant beings affected to determine if an action is good or evil. The essential utilitarian principle does not merely say that benefiting morally significant beings is good; it says that what provides the greatest net benefit for the greatest number of them is good.

Act Utilitarian Calculations

Utilitarians assume that benefit is a good thing and that harm is bad. On that basis they claim that people ought to maximize benefit and minimize harm for as many morally significant beings as possible. To discover actions that produce a net benefit, this ethical theory utilizes calculations of benefits against harms, benefits against alternative benefits, and harms against alternative harms.

Here is a simplified example of act utilitarian ethical evaluation. Suppose that a management team decides not to upgrade the safety of a new model of automobile by adding a certain part that would provide greater protection for the fuel tank. If they do not add the part, they believe they will save money. Because they want to make as much money as possible, they decide not to add the part. As time goes by, people are killed in low-speed accidents who would not have been killed if the part had been added.

Years later we might look back on that decision and its consequences to determine if the decision was ethical. First we would identify the significant consequences and divide them into harms and benefits. The significant benefits were that the company saved about $18 million during the six years that the car remained unaltered. The company also was able to save the $1 million it would have cost to alter the assembly lines so that the part could have been added. A final benefit is that each car was finished two minutes faster than if the part had been included, which meant that over the years more cars were built. Assume that this produced another $2 million in profits. The significant harms were that during the six years thirty people were killed in low-speed crashes who would have survived if the part had been added. Another sixty people were seriously injured or burned. The relatives and friends of the victims suffered because of the deaths and injuries. Fifty vehicles were destroyed by fire. The company spent $50 million to settle lawsuits connected to the deaths and injuries. The company's reputation was temporarily damaged, and it lost $5 million in profits because of the lower sales associated with the poor reputation.

After identifying the consequences, we would try to decide whether the benefits outweigh the harms or vice versa. In this case it is easy to see that the harms outweigh the benefits: the company lost more money than it saved, people were killed and injured, their friends and families suffered, vehicles were destroyed, and the company's reputation was damaged. There is nothing on the benefit side to outweigh these consequences. Therefore, a utilitarian would conclude that it was unethical for the managers to decide not to upgrade the safety of the fuel system.

This sample of a utilitarian analysis is incomplete and simplistic, but a more complete treatment would reach the same conclusion. According to Bentham, a complete utilitarian analysis would have to look beyond the obvious harms and benefits. Bentham discusses seven aspects of a utilitarian evaluation: intensity, duration, certainty, propinquity, fecundity, purity, and extent.

First, the agent must consider the intensity or significance of the harms and benefits, which I did to some extent in the example. The deaths were a very significant occurrence, and it would require a lot of benefit to outweigh them. Mill suggests that when we weigh the significance of competing benefits or harms the more significant aspect is the one that a competent agent would prefer. Contrary to Mill, one might also argue that the significance is inherent in the benefits and harms. This controversy did not arise in the automobile example because it was clear that the harms outweighed the benefits.

Second, the duration of each harm and benefit must be considered. A minor pain that lasts for years is more of a harm than a serious pain that is over in a couple of seconds. In my example the deaths had the consequences of greatest duration because these people were deprived of lives that might have lasted many years. None of the other factors were that far-reaching.

A third factor mentioned by Bentham is certainty: the certainty that the consequences we anticipate will follow from the action actually do so. In the automobile example I was looking back on this action with something approaching total knowledge. Certainty was not an important factor because I was certain about all the occurrences. I did not have to predict the consequences; I knew what they were.

A fourth consideration is what Bentham called propinquity. How remote is the harm or benefit? How soon will we experience the consequences? Bentham thought that an immediate harm was worse than one that would not happen for a long time. Once again, because I was looking back at the management decision, this aspect is not vital.

A fifth factor is the fecundity of the consequences; that is, how likely is it that the action will produce future benefits? An action that will promote future benefits is better than one that will not do so. In the automobile example there were no future benefits.

A sixth factor is the purity of the consequences. How likely is it that the action will produce future harm? In my example future harm was not relevant because I had already identified all the harms that had occurred over time.

The last factor is the extent or number of people affected by the harms and benefits. In the management case, I tried to identify the extent of the consequences.

We can see that although act utilitarianism grows out of a relatively simple insight about harm and benefit, it becomes complicated when we try to identify all of the harms and benefits connected to an action and all of the morally significant beings affected by it. Utilitarian calculations are often difficult to carry out. In some cases they can be performed completely. In other cases, such as the automobile example, we can produce a reasonable conclusion with which most people would agree.

Act Utilitarianism and the Traditional Ethical Assumptions

Act utilitarianism accepts the traditional ethical assumptions. It would claim that ethics is rational. We can use reason to reach theoretical and practical conclusions about ethics. We can provide reasons to support our ethical evaluations and our solutions to moral problems, and these reasons and solutions can be evaluated. Some reasons and solutions will be better than others. Utilitarians believe that people who share an ethical framework can discuss moral problems and arrive at mutually acceptable solutions. There is even some ground where act utilitarians can agree with proponents of competing ethical theories.

Act utilitarians enthusiastically endorse the view that all persons (full-status morally significant beings) are moral equals. They treat persons as moral equals because identical benefits count the same no matter who is the beneficiary: a benefit to a stranger counts as much as a benefit to a family member, or even to you. As Mill said, utilitarianism requires a moral agent "to be as strictly impartial as a disinterested and benevolent spectator."[4] Act utilitarians must maximize benefit for the greatest number of morally significant beings. When they are doing this, all people are moral equals. This means that there may be times when you must act contrary to your own self-interest to be ethical. Think about the CD example from Chapter 1: I want to buy a few new CDs for my collection, but I already have a couple hundred of them. Instead of buying the CDs, I could donate the money to a legitimate charity that would use it to cure some people from potentially fatal diseases. I may want to buy the CDs, but the ethical thing to do is to donate the money to the charity. The benefit of saving the lives will outweigh the pleasure I get from listening to the CDs. I must remember that even though the sick people are strangers, they are my moral equals. Therefore, if I want to be moral, I should help them.

Act utilitarianism also accepts the idea of universalizing ethical judgments. As in the previous example, if it is ethical for me to donate the money to a legitimate charity, then it is the ethical thing for anyone to do in the same situation. Assuming that we can identify sufficiently similar situations, we can universalize our ethical judgments.

Act Utilitarianism and the Basic Ethical Themes

Act utilitarianism has a position on each of the four basic ethical themes discussed in Chapter 1. The first theme is represented by the question: Are some actions, beliefs, or values always either good or evil? Utilitarians believe that specific actions are objectively good or evil. Individual actions or groups of related actions that cause more net harm than benefit are objectively evil. For example, the murder of millions of Jewish people by the Nazis during the thirties and forties was objectively evil because the harm of murdering these innocent people far outweighed any benefits for the Nazis. Act utilitarians focus on specific actions but point out that there are classes of actions wherein the harm or benefit might always outweigh the other factor. For example, raping and murdering a person would always seem to cause more harm than benefit. As Mill points out in *Utilitarianism,* we do not have to recalculate everything. Sometimes the verdict of human experience is so clear that we know the answer without actually doing the calculation.

Another significant theme in ethics is indicated by the question: What makes something good or evil; is it the consequences that are produced or the reasoning that led up to it? Utilitarians are ethical consequentialists who believe that the goodness or badness of something is a result of the consequences that are brought about by it. The reasoning is secondary for a utilitarian; our reasons are good if we intend to bring about beneficial consequences. However, an action that was meant to benefit someone might turn out to be bad if it actually causes harm.

The third theme relates to the question: Should we faithfully follow general rules of behavior, or should we separately evaluate each action and belief? In theory act utilitarians evaluate each action separately, but, as was mentioned in connection with the first theme, for some classes of actions the harm always seems to outweigh the benefit or vice versa. In relation to such classes of actions, utilitarians could save time by making use of ethical rules that articulate the "verdict of human experience." Of course, act utilitarians should always be open to the possibility of an exception to the rule if in a particular case disregarding the rule maximized net benefit. There might be cases where it is not wrong to kill, steal, lie, or break promises (e.g., if keeping a promise to someone would cause that person great harm). The ultimate focus for act utilitarians is on specific actions, but they can use rules as timesaving devices.

The fourth theme is connected to the proper focus of ethical attention: Should the group, community, or majority of persons be the focus of ethics, or should the focus be on the individual? Utilitarians believe that the focus of ethics should be the greatest good for the greatest number of people. In some cases utilitarians would sacrifice the individual for the greater good of the group because the good of the larger number of people outweighs the good of the individual. We believe that automobiles are an ethical product for a business to produce even though thousands of people are killed in automobile accidents each year. The enormous benefit of automobiles outweighs the deaths of these people. Act utilitarianism focuses on the group, not the individual, and promotes the greatest good or benefit for the greatest number of people.

Contrasting Act Utilitarianism with Ethical Relativism

Act utilitarianism is very different from ethical relativism (see Appendix 1). The basic ethical guideline identified by act utilitarianism is the utilitarian principle that bases good and evil on benefit and harm. Ethical relativism bases considerations of good and evil on the moral guidelines of actual societies. Act utilitarianism accepts all aspects of the traditional ethical assumptions; ethical relativism rejects one of them, moral equality. The two theories disagree on three of the four ethical themes. Whereas ethical relativism rejects objective moral judgments, act utilitarianism believes they exist. In relation to the second ethical theme, ethical relativism focuses on the ethical reasoning that precedes an action, whereas act utilitarianism looks at consequences. Ethical relativism mainly concentrates on following general rules; act utilitarianism centers on specific actions. Finally, the two theories hold similar beliefs with regard to the final theme—both focus ethical attention on the group, not the individual. Act utilitarianism does not have the problems that are found in ethical relativism, but it does have its own problems.

Problems with Act Utilitarianism

Act utilitarianism identifies the utilitarian principle as the basic ethical guideline and asserts that this guideline is better than others. This fundamental ethical guideline would prohibit the unlimited pursuit of self-interest. Although act utilitarianism satisfies the first three criteria for a successful ethical theory, it has difficulty with criterion four: The theory must help us to solve ethical problems. I will discuss several of the problems connected to act utilitarianism, relate them to criterion four, and provide brief utilitarian responses to them.

Doing the Calculations

The first problem with act utilitarianism is the difficulty connected to doing the utilitarian calculations. If we cannot successfully do the calculations, the theory cannot help us to solve ethical problems. This problem with the calculations has three main aspects.

First, it is hard to identify all the consequences of an action. An accurate utilitarian analysis must go beyond the immediate consequences and find all the results. This is a difficult undertaking. Short-range consequences can be difficult to identify, and long-range consequences are even harder to identify, especially when you are trying to predict them before the action has happened. In the fictional automobile example in this chapter, we were looking back over time and therefore could identify the results with some accuracy. If we had to try to decide in advance whether the act was ethical, it would be much harder because we would have to predict future consequences. With accurate and extensive information we can make reasonable predictions about the future, but such predictions are never guaranteed to be correct. In addition, how can we be sure we have extended our search for consequences far enough into the future? Assume that there is a great public outcry after the automobile case. The public begins to put pressure on legislators to improve automobile safety, and legislators put pressure on the National Highway and Traffic Safety Administration (NHTSA). After a year of study, the NHTSA issues a regulation to prevent this kind of safety problem in the future. Is this a consequence of the decision of the managers to not improve the safety of their automobiles? If so, does it change our ethical evaluation of that case? This question would be difficult to answer in a satisfactory way. An ethical theory should help us to solve moral problems, but sometimes difficulties with doing the calculations will interfere with act utilitarianism accomplishing this objective.

The second aspect of the problem is that it is difficult to weigh harms and benefits when they are very different kinds of things. Imagine that if the NHTSA mandates a certain safety feature for automobiles it will save twenty lives a year but cost American car buyers $100 million. How do we weigh twenty lives against $100 million? We place a high value on human life, but is it worth $5 million to save a life? Perhaps we really cannot even make a reasonable judgment about this matter unless we know what would be done with the $100 million. If people will spend it to improve their lives, will they improve them sufficiently to balance the loss of twenty lives? Utilitarians depend on calculations, but the elements that must be weighed are sometimes impossible to compare. Once again, this will make it hard to solve some ethical problems.

The final aspect of the problem is less serious than the others. Act utilitarians would have to spend a lot of their time identifying harms and benefits and weighing them. The utilitarian calculations might take up an enormous amount of our time, making solving ethical problems very time-consuming. This difficulty coupled with the previous two aspects of the problem suggest that the utilitarian theory will only be partially successful at meeting criterion four. In relatively simple and clear-cut cases, we will be able to do the calculations, but in other cases, we will have trouble.

Utilitarians would respond to the difficulty of doing the calculations by stating that this "problem" is inevitable in any ethical theory that takes seriously the context and all the aspects of an ethical problem. Unless we want to oversimplify the moral problem, we must look at its context and various aspects. When we do this, the calculations will be hard to do. This response clearly does not solve the problem but claims that this problem is inevitable with any consequentialist theory that does not oversimplify matters.

Their response to the problem of noncomparability would be the same; that is, act utilitarians would say this is also inevitable. In life we need to make hard decisions where the competing factors are very different. Act utilitarianism provides an overriding value—benefit to morally significant beings—to allow us to attempt to make such decisions. It may be difficult to determine whether there is more benefit in saving twenty lives or $100 million, but what better way is there to make a decision about this matter? Utilitarians would argue that at least they provide reasonable guidance for the decision-making process, even if it is still difficult to carry it out. Once again, the response does not solve the problem but merely claims it is inevitable in this kind of theory.

The act utilitarian response to the problem about the time required to do the calculations was answered by Mill when he stated that we do not have to calculate everything. Sometimes the verdict of human experience is so clear that we know the answer without actually doing the calculation. In many cases you will not have to do the calculations because you know the answer due to previous experience. In other cases you will have to do the work if you are interested in being ethical; but why should we assume that being ethical should be easy and take very little time? This response provides a partial solution to the problem because we will not have to do the calculations in every case.

Injustice

Another serious problem, one relating to criterion four, is that act utilitarianism focuses on the majority or group and is willing to sacrifice a minority if it would bring about the greatest good of the greatest number of people. This leads to injustice, and critics claim that a theory that permits injustice does not really help us solve moral problems. Although the "solution" may be ethical in a utilitarian sense, it is unjust in a wider sense. Such a contradictory solution does not seem to be satisfactory for critics of utilitarianism. Furthermore, this injustice is particularly disturbing if you are a member of the minority that is being treated unjustly. It might balance out if sometimes you were part of the majority and were benefited and at other times were part of the minority and were harmed. However, it is also possible that you might always end up in the minority; thus, you would always suffer harm to benefit the majority. It seems unjust that some minority should always be sacrificed for the good of the majority. Utilitarianism might produce results that are unjust in many cases. For example, cheating on a test is by definition unfair or unjust. However, it would be ethical for a utilitarian to cheat if the net benefit was maximized. To cite a more complicated and controversial example, I think it was unjust that about 200 thousand civilians were killed in Hiroshima and Nagasaki to bring about a quicker ending to World War II and make it unnecessary for the Allied forces to invade

Japan. Most people would agree that it is fair or just to kill combatants in a war (and it may even be fair or just to kill noncombatants who are directly supporting the war effort, such as working in munitions factories), but it is unfair or unjust to kill noncombatants or civilians (who are not directly supporting the war effort). Many Japanese civilians in these cities had no direct role in supporting the war effort, and it was unjust to kill them. Critics charge that utilitarianism is a poor moral theory because it produces many "ethical" solutions that are unjust. Therefore, act utilitarianism is not really helping us to solve ethical problems in a satisfactory manner.

The utilitarian response to this criticism is that the critics have one idea of justice and utilitarians have a different one (although this seems wrong in the cheating case). For utilitarians justice is treating morally significant beings as moral equals and counting their harm and benefit no differently from that of any other morally significant beings. It is because of moral equality or "utilitarian justice" that on some occasions we must do horrible things and sacrifice persons for the greater good. The utilitarians try to get us to focus on the benefit to the majority rather than on the harm to the minority. This response does not solve the problem for me; it merely highlights it. I think this issue represents the most significant dispute between act utilitarianism and theories that protect the individual, such as the moral rights theory. This will be discussed further in the last chapter.

Moral Luck

The final problem undercuts the ability of act utilitarianism to help us solve ethical problems. If good and evil depend on the consequences of an action, then the ability to perform good actions is not totally in the control of the moral agent. An element of luck enters the moral realm.[5] Imagine that I send a check to a charity but that the check is permanently lost in the mail. No beneficial consequences resulted from my action, and therefore the action was not good. In a sense my bad luck prevented me from performing a good action. When I realize that the check has never been cashed, I can cancel it and send another one—but that is a different check and a different action.

Many philosophers believe that the ability to perform good actions should be completely in the control of the moral agent; they reject consequentialist theories for this reason. This problem relates to the fourth criterion for evaluating ethical theories. When I mailed my check, I thought I had solved my ethical problem. I had given money to charity and had done the ethical thing. It turns out that I had not really solved the problem in the way that I thought; I had not done anything ethical. Because consequences can never be guaranteed beforehand, utilitarian theory does not always help us to solve ethical problems.

Utilitarians would respond to this problem in a similar way to the one regarding the calculations. This is an inevitable aspect of a consequentialist theory. The reason consequentialist theories have these problems is because they do not oversimplify ethical problems. As I noted concerning the earlier problem, this is not a solution and shows that utilitarianism will not always be a successful ethical theory.

Rule Utilitarianism

When moral philosophers understand the problems associated with act utilitarianism, some of them turn to a different form of utilitarianism, called rule utilitarianism. Rule utilitarianism does not solve all the problems with act utilitarianism, but it does seem to solve the problem of injustice—that unjust things like cheating on tests or killing civilians would be ethical if they maximized net benefit. Rule utilitarianism is also a consequentialist ethical theory, but it examines the consequences of generally following moral rules rather than focusing on the consequences of specific actions. The ethical standard for rule utilitarianism might be phrased: *It is good for persons to act from those moral rules, the general following of which would promote the greatest net benefit for the greatest number of morally significant beings; it is bad for persons to act from rules, the general following of which would promote the greatest net harm for the greatest number of morally significant beings.* Based on this standard, an action will be good if it follows from a legitimate moral rule that generally maximizes benefits for the greatest number of persons.

Rule utilitarians claim that we can identify a "rule" to guide any morally significant action. Suppose I send some money to a charity because I believe everyone ought to help those who are less fortunate. The complete description of the action ought to include identification of the rule that guided it. For example, I performed the action—giving this money to this charity—because I thought I should act in accord with my rule: everyone ought to help those who are less fortunate. The action will be ethical if it follows from the right kind of rule, one whose general following would maximize net benefit for those affected by persons following it. If the general following of the rule "everyone ought to help those who are less fortunate," would produce more net benefit than harm for those affected by persons following it, then it is a legitimate moral rule, and we should follow it if we want to be ethical. Thus, rule utilitarianism has two aspects: (1) we should determine the legitimate moral rules that maximize net benefit for those affected by the general following of them and follow these moral rules without exceptions, and (2) if contemplating whether or not to perform an action, we should do so only if it would follow from a legitimate moral rule.

Rule utilitarians must follow legitimate moral rules without exceptions or they would become act utilitarians. An exception would be a particular case where breaking the rule would maximize net benefit in that specific case. Rule utilitarians would not do this because they do not examine the consequences in particular cases. If they examined particular cases and broke their rules in every case where violating the rule would maximize net benefit, they would be no different from act utilitarians and would not be able to avoid the problem with injustice. Rule utilitarians do acknowledge that situations may change. When they do, new rules may be needed because following them will produce more net human benefit than following the old rules. For example, perhaps at one time the general following of the rule "it is unethical to get a divorce" maximized human benefit. If conditions change and things become easier for divorced people (especially single parents), then a new moral rule may be necessary. The inability to make exceptions to moral rules is the essential difference between rule and act utilitarianism. As was mentioned earlier, act utilitarians can use moral rules as timesaving devices, but they must always consider the possibility that an exception will maximize net benefit.

Rule utilitarianism solves the problem with justice because it makes cheating, stealing, and possibly even killing civilians unethical. For example, the general following of the rule "it is unethical to cheat on tests" would produce more net benefit than harm for those affected. If everyone cheats on tests, there will be an enormous amount of harm. Tests will become meaningless, and educators will lose this valuable tool for assessing students. Therefore, the rule is a legitimate moral rule, and we should follow it without exceptions. Cheating is both unethical and unjust. Rule utilitarians do not get contradictory results on these issues.

Rule utilitarianism also diminishes the problem with moral luck. Luck is less of a factor in the consequences of the general following of moral rules than in specific cases. Even though my check to a charity may not get there, and hence sending the check does not produce any beneficial consequences, in general checks usually get to charities. Even with occasional bad luck, the moral rule that "it is ethical for affluent people to help those in need" would maximize net benefit.

Rule utilitarianism will not alleviate the first two aspects of the problem connected to difficulties with doing the calculation. In fact, it will be more difficult to identify all the consequences connected to the general following of a moral rule than to distinguish those resulting from a specific action. It is impossible to know all the consequences of the general following of the rule "it is unethical to ever kill civilians in wartime"; we could only guess whether or not this would produce a net benefit. If it is impossible to calculate all of the consequences of some potential moral rules, then rule utilitarianism can have only limited success in helping us solve moral problems. We would not be able to determine the complete set of legitimate moral rules, but we may be able to sufficiently identify the consequences of some moral rules and evaluate them. Rule utilitarianism also does not alleviate the problem with regard to weighing very different kinds of consequences, such as large sums of money against lives. On this issue both versions of utilitarianism are equally problematic.

Rule utilitarianism is an improvement over act utilitarianism in a couple of areas, but it is less successful in identifying the consequences that result from following a general rule as opposed to those that are produced by a specific action. There is another serious complaint that act utilitarians would bring against rule utilitarianism. If we are really interested in maximizing net human benefit, act utilitarians claim that we would be foolish not to make an exception to a rule when that exception would maximize benefit in a specific case and have no wider implications. They consider rule utilitarians unwise for blindly following moral rules and for never being willing to consider even the most beneficial exceptions. To balance out the problems with injustice and moral luck, act utilitarians would contend that their version of utilitarianism will actually produce more net benefit and less net harm.

Conclusion

Act utilitarianism has two main strengths, both related to this basic ethical insight: Something is bad if it harms someone; if it helps or benefits someone, it is good. First, it gives ethics a content—harm and benefit to morally significant beings. It allows people to look at the consequences of their actions, and many people believe that consequences are vital to ethics. Second, this ethical theory responds to the particular situation faced by the moral agent. Act utilitarians evaluate each action separately instead of trying to rigidly follow a set of moral rules.

In regard to the criteria for evaluating ethical theories, act utilitarianism is only a partially successful ethical theory. It does produce a basic ethical guideline. It does argue that this ethical guideline is better than others, and it does produce an ethical guideline that would prohibit the unlimited pursuit of self-interest. However, act utilitarianism has limited success in helping us solve ethical problems because there are problems related to doing the utilitarian calculations. The theory will only allow us to solve ethical problems in relatively simple cases. There is also the serious problem involving the conflict between what many people think is just and what utilitarians claim is ethical. Finally, there is the problem with moral luck; being ethical is not completely under the control of the moral agent. We will now turn to a Kantian ethical theory that does not have any of these problems.

QUESTIONS FOR REVIEW

Here are some questions to help you review the main concepts in this chapter.

1. What is the essential principle or standard of act utilitarianism?
2. What is the justification for using this standard?
3. How do act utilitarians divide the morally significant from what is not morally significant?
4. What are necessary and sufficient conditions or attributes? Can we successfully use "benefit" and "harm" even without knowing the necessary and sufficient attributes for each?
5. What two amendments should be added to the initial intuition that benefiting people is good and harming them is bad?
6. What were the six most significant benefits and harms in the automobile safety case? If these were the only consequences, what ethical conclusion would you reach about the decision not to upgrade the safety of the fuel tank?
7. What position does act utilitarianism take on each of the three traditional ethical assumptions?
8. What views does act utilitarianism endorse on each of the four ethical themes?
9. Identify one similarity and two differences between act utilitarianism and ethical relativism?
10. What do you think is the most significant problem with act utilitarianism? Why? Why is act utilitarianism only a partially successful ethical theory?

NOTES

1. Peter Singer, *Practical Ethics* (Cambridge, MA: Cambridge University Press, 1993), p. 57.

2. Ibid., p. 131.

3. Mary Anne Warren, "On the Moral and Legal Status of Abortion," in *Morality in Practice,* edited by James P. Sterba (Belmont, CA: Wadsworth, 1997), p. 139.

4. John Stuart Mill, *Utilitarianism* (Indianapolis, IN: Hackett Publishing Company, 1979), p. 16.

5. See Bernard Williams, "Moral Luck," in *Moral Luck: Philosophical Papers, 1973–1980* (Cambridge, MA: Cambridge University Press, 1981).

Chapter 4

Kantian Ethical Theory

Most people who drive automobiles occasionally exceed the posted speed limits, but assume you have an acquaintance who never does this. You ask the person why he or she never speeds, and the answer is, "I'm afraid I'll be caught by the police and have to pay a fine." This would be a consequentialist approach to speeding. He or she does not speed because of the fear of bad consequences. There is, however, another answer that the person could give: "I do not speed because I respect the law. Sometimes I want to speed because I'm in a hurry, but because I respect the law I never do it." This is a very different answer; it is not concerned with either consequences or personal wants. The person's action is guided simply by respect for the law. It may seem odd that someone would respect the speeding laws, but assume that this person respects the law in general and therefore obeys all the laws, even the posted speed limits.

This example concerns the laws established by a government—the kind of law that in Chapter 1 I said needs to be separated from ethics. We know that this kind of law exists, but German philosopher Immanuel Kant (1724–1804) argues that another kind of law also exists, moral law. It is not the law of any one country or society; moral law applies to all persons or rational beings. In this chapter I discuss a deontological ethical theory centered around the idea of acting from respect for the moral law.

In Chapter 1, I suggested that philosophers often work with this model of action:

Reasoning → *Action* → *Consequences*

Consequentialist ethical theories like utilitarianism claim that good and evil are related to the consequences that result from an action. In contrast, *deontological ethical theories* focus on the reasoning that precedes the action. The word "deontology" relates to the Greek word "deon," which translates roughly as "duty." Duty is a very difficult concept. In this chapter I will avoid the term and simply talk about acting from respect for the moral law. Immanuel Kant is the most influential of the deontological philosophers, and his ethical theory is extremely complicated.[1] I will not provide an exact explication of his ideas but instead discuss a simplified "Kantian ethics" centered around acting from respect for the moral law.

Rules and Action

In the section on rule utilitarianism in Chapter 3 I discussed the relation between rules and actions. This reasoning is also essential to Kantian ethics: for any action, we can identify a personal rule that guides the action. Suppose that I send some money to a charity because I believe that everyone ought to help those who are less fortunate. My reasoning might be described as follows: I performed the action (giving money to this charity) because I thought I should act from my personal rule: Everyone ought to help those who are less fortunate. The Kantian idea is that every action is guided by a personal rule. If persons want to be ethical, the personal rules that guide their actions must be able to be willed to be moral laws. It is not enough that by coincidence personal rules of action are consistent with these moral laws, persons must be acting because they could will their personal rules to be moral laws.

The Basic Ethical Insights of Kantian Ethics

Kantian ethics is related to two basic ethical insights: (1) *persons are moral equals,* and (2) *our ethical treatment of persons in sufficiently similar situations ought to be consistent.* The moral law is connected to both of these. The additional idea that gives Kantian ethics its distinctive orientation is that to be ethical, persons must act from respect for the moral law. The idea of moral equality among persons means that all persons are equally bound by moral laws and that all persons count the same when we are applying moral laws. Assume that the rule "it is wrong to steal other people's property" can be willed to be a moral law. If persons are moral equals, they are all bound by the rule, and the rule protects all property. No one has a privileged ethical position that allows him or her to ignore the rule. Therefore, moral laws place obligations on everyone; that is, they are universal.

The ideas of moral equality and ethical consistency are connected. Suppose that the rule "it is wrong to steal other people's property" is legitimate. If I believe two persons are moral equals and that they are in sufficiently similar situations, then I ought to act from the moral rule in a consistent way—I should refrain from stealing either person's property. If I do not act this way, I am being inconsistent in two ways. The first inconsistency concerns the rule; I am not consistently acting from the rule. The rule orders me not to steal, but in one case I act from it and in a sufficiently similar case I disregard it. The second inconsistency relates to my attitude toward persons. I have said that persons are moral equals, but I treat them as if they were not moral equals, stealing from one and not from the other. Kantian ethics claims that persons ought to be consistent, both in acting from moral laws and in the treatment of persons. The ideas of moral equality and ethical consistency are key ethical insights behind Kantian ethics.

Persons and Moral Laws

Moral laws are perceived by persons as universal commands. Moral laws command persons universally or absolutely; they must be followed without exceptions. They are not conditional rules. Conditional rules tell us what actions persons should take to attain some desired goal and have an if-then form: If you want to lose weight, then you ought to exercise and watch what you eat. The rule is conditional because it will only guide you to act if you want to lose weight. Therefore, conditional rules do not obligate everyone—only those people who desire to reach the goal. In contrast, legitimate moral rules place an obligation on everyone regardless of his or her desires; they are universal.

It is rational for a person to act from the moral law. If a person violates the moral law, he or she has acted inconsistently or irrationally. Moral laws bind all persons because all persons are moral equals. Ethical conduct is only possible for free, rational beings: beings who are capable, at least, of deliberating, following rules, making decisions, and supporting those decisions with reasons. They must be able to understand the idea of the moral law and decide how to act based on reasoning about personal rules of action and moral laws. Finally, they must be able to act from respect for the moral law. If a being cannot meet these criteria, it will not qualify as a person under Kantian ethics.

The Ethical Standard of Kantian Ethics

Kantians use a basic moral principle or ethical standard, called the *Categorical Imperative,* to determine the legitimate rules that ought to guide action. The Categorical Imperative is similar to an essential principle in many religions. In Christianity this principle is called the Golden Rule. One version of the Golden Rule is, "Do unto others as you would have them do unto you." The first formulation of the Categorical Imperative or ethical standard might be phrased: *Act only from those personal rules that you can at the same time will to be moral laws.* The difference between the Golden Rule and the first formulation of the Kantian Categorical Imperative is subtle, yet important, because the Kantian formula is less likely to lead to a subjective interpretation. I might interpret the Golden Rule as telling me to treat persons the way I would like to be treated. This interpretation runs the risk of having someone understand it as the instruction to use his or her personal likes and dislikes as the ethical standard for how to treat everyone else. This would extend the person's subjective standard to everyone and would have the problems related to ethical subjectivism. In my opinion this is not what was meant by the Golden Rule, and it is certainly not what Kant meant. Persons are to act from those personal rules that they could will to be ethical laws because they are rational, moral equals. The first formulation is related to the idea that the moral law is universal. Presumably the two features, rationality (consistency) and moral equality would lead persons to will the same set of moral laws. If they follow the Categorical Imperative and act on personal rules that they could will to be moral laws, they will have acted ethically.

Kantian ethical theory identifies another version of the Kantian ethical standard that also relates to consistency and moral equality. The second formulation of the Categorical Imperative might be stated as: *Act in regard to all persons in ways that treat them as ends in themselves and never simply as means to accomplish the ends of others.* Persons are free, rational beings who have various purposes and goals that they wish to accomplish. The second formulation of the Categorical Imperative or ethical standard acknowledges these characteristics when it refers to persons as ends in themselves. Kantian ethics demands that persons evaluate their personal rules and act only on those that they could will to be universal laws. Persons must also acknowledge that other persons should do the same thing since they are moral equals. They must never forget that persons are free and can reason and act, and they should never treat them merely as tools to accomplish their goals, the way they would use a hammer to fix something. For example, I cannot simply order you to help me repair my roof and expect you to do it regardless of whatever plans you may have. This disregards your status as a free, rational being who can make decisions and has goals and instead treats you merely as a means for me to get my roof fixed. I need to ask you to help me fix my roof. This leaves the decision up to you and acknowledges your status as a free being who can make decisions and has his or her own goals. I am still using you as a means to get my roof repaired, but not merely as a means. Rational beings can use persons to accomplish their ends, but they should never use them merely as means to accomplish those ends. Persons are moral equals and, therefore, must act only from personal rules that treat persons as ends in themselves, and never from rules that treat persons merely as means to accomplish their ends. If they do this, they will have acted ethically.

Legitimate Moral Laws

How are persons to know the rules that they should will to be moral laws? To answer this question, Kantian ethics appeals to consistency and moral equality. First, they must determine the personal rule on which they propose to act. Second, they should only act from rules that are internally consistent. Third, they should only follow rules that are universal and that treat persons as moral equals. Fourth, they should never act from rules that treat persons merely as means to accomplish the ends of others.

Consider this proposed rule: "I may promise to do something and then break that promise if it is in my self-interest to do so." Assume that I may break the promise for any self-interested reason, no matter how trivial. Therefore, based on willing this rule to be a moral law, everyone would make promises and then in many cases break them. This rule does not meet the first criterion because it is internally inconsistent. When I promise to do something, perhaps help you fix your roof, I am saying that I *will* do it. However, this rule is also stating that I *will not* do it if something trivial, but in my self-interest, arises. It is saying that I *will* help you fix your roof and that I *will not* help you. These two aspects of the rule are inconsistent and would make my promise to help you fix your roof meaningless. If this rule were extended to guide all promises, it would make promises in general meaningless. Thus, this rule would not meet the first criterion because it is internally inconsistent.

Rational beings should also reject potential rules that do not treat persons as moral equals. Because we are moral equals, legitimate moral laws apply to all of us. A rule may be rejected if it is not universal, that is, if it does not apply to everyone. Suppose someone proposes the rule that "only women should help those less fortunate than themselves." This rule should be rejected because it is not universal; it does not apply to all persons. The rule implies that women have a special ethical standing, but this is incorrect if all persons are moral equals. All legitimate moral laws treat persons as moral equals and hence apply to everyone. To be ethical, persons must follow only rules that they could will to be moral laws.

There are many rules that Kantians believe could be willed to be moral laws. One is that "persons ought to keep their promises." Keeping all of our promises is internally consistent because the rule, by its formulation, does not interfere with our doing that to which we have obligated ourselves. There might be a promise that is foolishly made—one which it turns out the person does not have the ability to keep—but the inability to keep this promise is a problem with the particular promise and not a necessary problem with the moral rule. This moral rule also treats persons as moral equals because persons will be keeping their promises to everyone, rather than keeping them to some persons and not to others. Finally, it does not treat persons merely as means; by keeping my promise to someone, I respect the person's ends that may be related to the promise. Therefore, persons can will the rule to be a moral law.

Another example would be the rule that "it is unethical to enslave persons." This rule could be willed to be a moral law because it is internally consistent and would treat persons as moral equals and ends in themselves. Slaves meet the criteria as persons, but they are not treated as persons (as free, rational beings and moral equals). They are treated merely as means to satisfy the ends of their owners. If we claimed that slavery were ethical, we would be claiming that some persons (rational beings) ought not to be treated as persons (rational beings). This would be inconsistent and would violate the idea that rational beings must treat persons as moral equals. Conversely, the rule that slavery is unethical supports the idea that persons must always be treated as rational beings and moral equals, and as ends in themselves.

There is no other method to determine the rules that should guide action. Kantians cannot claim that the moral laws would be the rules that produce the best consequences. This is the position taken by rule utilitarianism (Chapter 3). According to rule utilitarians, we should follow rules that maximize net human benefit for the greatest number of persons. In contrast, Kantians claim that the legitimacy of moral laws is not connected to consequences. Therefore, the Kantian ethical standard does not specify the kind of consequences that must be produced. The rules that persons should will to be moral laws ought to be rules that fit the two criteria of consistency and moral equality.

Kantian ethics would not provide a complete list of all the rules that could be willed to be moral laws. As rational beings, persons ought to evaluate their personal rules of action. It would be inconsistent and unethical to reject being a rational being and not to evaluate those personal rules. Of course, Kantians believe that if persons use reason correctly they will all arrive at the same conclusions about which rules could be willed to be moral laws. The emphasis, however, is on the moral standard and the procedure used to identify the legitimate rules to guide action, not on identifying a specific set of moral laws.

When a person contemplates a morally significant action, he or she must be able to identify or arrive at a description of the action. From the description, the personal rule that would guide the action can be identified. For example, suppose that my contemplated action is helping you fix your roof, which is related to my promise to help you fix your roof. The rule that would guide my action if I help you is, "persons ought to keep their promises." As discussed earlier, this rule could be willed to be a moral law; therefore, it is ethical for me to help you fix your roof. We would have to be able to know what counted and did not count as making a promise, the relevant personal rule, and whether that rule could be willed to be a moral law. In some cases there may be more than one relevant rule. If both rules could be willed to be moral laws, the action is ethical. However, if one rule could be willed to be a moral law and the other could not, there would be a conflict. Conflicts between rules will be discussed further in the section on the problems with Kantian ethics.

Justification and Determining the Morally Significant

Some aspects of the justification for the Kantian ethical standard, or Categorical Imperative, have been mentioned in earlier sections, but I will bring them together here. The first version of the Categorical Imperative or ethical standard states: *Act only from those personal rules that you can at the same time will to be moral laws.* The justification for this ethical standard is connected to the idea that moral laws must be universal if persons are moral equals. If moral laws are universal, then all persons must act from them. If a person does not act from the moral law, he or she is not acting consistently or rationally. Persons are capable of being rational and ought to act rationally, presumably out of respect for their rationality. Ultimately, acting from respect for the moral law is based on acting from respect for rationality. If someone now asks, "Why should rational beings act from respect for their rationality?" there is no compelling answer. As Kant himself acknowledged, persons are imperfectly rational beings. Why should imperfectly rational beings strive to be perfectly rational beings? Why does the capacity to be rational force us to act from respect for that rationality? Perhaps the only answer is that it is a basic premise of Kantian ethics that persons are rational beings and that they ought to act from respect for their rationality.

The second formulation of the Categorical Imperative, or Kantian ethical standard, is: *Act in regard to all persons in ways that treat them as ends in themselves and never simply as means to accomplish the ends of others.* The justification for this ethical standard relates to persons being centers of reasoning and action and having various purposes and goals that they wish to accomplish. In other words, they are ends in themselves. If persons are ends in themselves but are not treated as such, it would be inconsistent and irrational. Therefore, if persons do not endorse the second formulation of the Categorical Imperative as the legitimate ethical standard, they are being irrational. The reason for endorsing the second version of the Categorical Imperative is ultimately the same as the reason for supporting the first version: persons ought to act rationally because they ought to act from respect for their rationality.

The legitimate ethical standard identified by Kantians provides a means of separating the morally significant from what is not morally significant. With respect to actions, any action performed from respect for the moral law is morally significant. It is also morally significant if we fail to act from respect for the moral law; for example, acting on self-interest in a situation relevant to a legitimate moral law would also be morally significant. If I see a small child drowning in a shallow pond, I ought to wade in and save the child even if I do not want to get my clothes wet. It is morally significant if I fail to do this. In general, in Kantian ethics anything related to acting from respect for the moral law is morally significant.

Kantian Ethics and the Traditional Ethical Assumptions

Kantian ethics accepts the traditional ethical assumptions. It would claim that ethics is rational. We can use reason to reach theoretical and practical conclusions about ethics. We can also provide reasons to support moral laws and solutions to ethical problems, evaluate those reasons and solutions, and conclude that some of them are better than others. More specifically, we can evaluate personal rules and see if we could will them to be moral laws. Kantians would also agree that there are mutually acceptable solutions to moral problems, assuming we agree on the description of the proposed action and on the evaluation of the proposed rule.

Kantian ethics also accepts the view that all persons are moral equals. All persons are moral equals means that all persons are bound by the moral law. If "breaking a promise is unethical" is a moral law, then all persons ought to keep their promises to everyone. No one has a special moral status that allows him or her to break promises and still be ethical.

Finally, Kantian ethics endorses the idea of universalizing moral judgments. If one person can legitimately will the rule "breaking a promise is unethical" to be a moral law, then any rational being can do so, and it would be unethical to break promises. The moral law applies equally to all of us. Assuming that we can will some rules to be moral laws, we can universalize our ethical evaluations connected to those rules.

Kantian Ethics and the Four Ethical Themes

Kantian ethics has a position on each of the four basic ethical themes. The first theme is represented by the question: Are some actions, beliefs, or values always either good or evil? In other words, are some actions objectively good or evil? Kantians believe that specific actions that follow from the moral law are objectively good; other actions, which violate the moral law, are objectively evil. For example, enslaving persons would be objectively evil because it would treat persons merely as means to the masters' ends.

Another significant theme in ethics is indicated by the question: What makes something good or evil; is it the consequences that are produced or the reasoning that leads up to it? Kantian ethics asserts that the rightness or wrongness of something depends on the reasoning that guided it. The ethical evaluation of an action depends on whether or not the action was done because the personal rule that guided it could be willed to be a moral law.

The third theme is related to the question: Should we faithfully follow general rules of behavior, or should we separately evaluate each action and belief? Kantians believe ethics involves following rules that could be willed to be moral laws. They allow no exceptions to acting from these rules, because making an exception would mean that we have been inconsistent in acting from the moral law or that we have not treated persons as moral equals.

The fourth theme is connected to the proper focus of ethical attention: Should the group, community, or majority of persons be the focus of ethics, or should the focus be on the individual? Kantians believe that the focus of ethics should be the individual person or rational being. Each person must evaluate his or her personal rules of action and act from those that he or she could will to be moral laws. If individuals use reason correctly, however, everyone will arrive at the same set of legitimate rules of action.

Contrasting Kantian Ethics with Act Utilitarianism

Kantian ethical theory and act utilitarianism have some similarities (see Appendix 1). Both theories accept the traditional ethical assumptions. Both believe ethics is rational, that people are moral equals, and that some moral judgments can be universalized. Both theories are also objectivist ethical theories because they claim that some actions are always good or evil.

These ethical theories do have their differences however. Act utilitarians identify the utilitarian principle as the basic ethical guideline, whereas Kantians identify the two versions of the Categorical Imperative as the fundamental ethical guidelines. According to Kantians, the reasoning that precedes an action rather than the consequences that follow it makes the action good or evil. This view eliminates the element of luck present in consequentialist theories and places the ability to act ethically completely in the control of the moral agent. Another important difference is that act utilitarians evaluate actions on a case-by-case basis, whereas Kantians follow general rules. Stealing is always wrong for a Kantian, but an act utilitarian may identify some cases where the benefits of stealing something outweighs its harms. The third major difference between the theories is that Kantian ethics focuses on the individual moral agent evaluating personal rules and acting from those that could be willed to be moral laws. Act utilitarianism is oriented toward obtaining the greatest benefit for the majority of persons.

Problems with Kantian Ethics

Kantian ethical theory identifies ethical guidelines and argues that these guidelines are better than those of other theories. The guidelines identified by the theory would prevent the unlimited pursuit of self-interest. The problems with Kantian ethics relate to the fourth criterion for a successful ethical theory: The theory must help us to solve ethical problems. I will discuss a few of the problems with Kantian ethics.

Descriptions for Actions

The first main difficulty relates to the procedure for creating moral laws. Persons must be able to identify an action ("making a promise" or "killing an innocent person") and then decide on the rule that guides the action ("persons ought to keep their promises" or "it is unethical to kill innocent people"). This identification is essential because without it there will be no personal rule. Without the personal rule, there will be no way to determine ethical action since an action will only be ethical if it follows from a personal rule that could be willed to be a moral law. Kant seems to have assumed that there is only one correct description for an action and that each action only connects to one rule. Examples suggest otherwise. Suppose I contemplate taking some food from a grocery store to feed my starving children. What is the correct description of the action? Is it a case of stealing, of saving the lives of innocent people, or of caring for my children? There are certainly incorrect ways to describe this action (e.g., taking a walk in the park), but which of the plausible descriptions is the one to use in determining the appropriate rule and ultimately whether the action is ethical? If we cannot identify a single description for the action, we are faced with multiple personal rules. Is this the relevant rule? If I want my children to live, I ought to take the food. Is it this rule? It is unethical to steal the property of others. Is it this rule? Persons ought to try to save the lives of innocent people. Is it this rule? We ought to care for our children. It seems that all of these rules (and perhaps others) apply to the case. The problem is that we do not know the proper description or rule. If we cannot identify the single relevant personal rule, we will not be able to decide how to act ethically because we will not know what rule to examine to see if it can be willed to be a moral law. If we cannot do this, we will not obtain help in solving the relevant moral problem. Although this is a serious criticism, the theory would still work in areas where there is no question about the correct description of the action. This criticism shows that the theory will have limited success as an ethical theory.

Conflicting Moral Laws

One way to solve the problem of not being able to identify a single description and rule is to declare that several descriptions and rules are relevant to any action. This, however, creates a new dilemma, the problem of conflicting moral laws. Suppose a person could will both of these rules to be moral laws: (1) It is unethical to steal, and (2) Persons ought to try to save the lives of innocent persons. In a case where children are starving and the only way to get food is by theft, which rule should we follow? Kantian theory does not seem to allow us to rank moral laws; hence, we will not know what is the ethical thing to do. If persons do not know which rule to follow, they will not have help in solving moral problems. To the extent that conflicting rules arise, Kantian ethics will not be a successful ethical theory.[2]

Exceptions to Moral Laws

The third main problem with Kantian ethics is connected to the idea that Kantians allow no exceptions to moral laws. This problem also relates to criterion four, that the theory must help us to solve ethical problems. Using Kantian ethics, there can be no exceptions to legitimate moral laws because we must be consistent and treat persons as moral equals. Kant thought, for example, that persons should never lie, even if a lie might prevent someone from being hurt or even killed. This may seem ridiculous, but we must remember that Kantians are not concerned with consequences. They endorse respect for the moral law, not maximum benefit. When we disregard consequences, what could possibly motivate us to break our moral rule and lie? This aspect of the theory seems rigid and inflexible. If there can be no compromises, Kantian theory will not help us to solve many real moral problems.

In connection to this problem, there is a promising solution that Kantians could offer. They could claim that although moral laws need to be followed without exceptions there is no reason why the moral laws cannot have exceptions built into them. The rule might be: It is unethical to steal the property of others except when stealing is the only way to save the lives of innocent people. The only difficulty with this solution is that the exception built into the rule would have to be motivated by considerations related either to consistency or moral equality, and not to consequences. We might argue that we can incorporate this exception about saving the lives of innocent people by stealing into the previous law out of respect for the moral equality of those people whose lives are in danger. Unfortunately, while respecting the moral equality of the people whose lives are in danger, we are not respecting the moral equality of the people from whom we are stealing. A main problem with these exceptions to the rules is that they bring us back to the problem of conflicting moral laws. Why is it more important, based on Kantian ethics, to respect moral equality related to life than moral equality connected to property? Without some policy concerning the relative moral value of ethical laws, this strategy is doomed to fail. Once again, we see a criticism that leads to the conclusion that Kantian ethical theory will only be partially successful in helping us to solve ethical problems.

Conclusion

The Kantian approach to ethics has been very influential. Many persons believe that moral equality is an important element in ethics, and no ethical theory takes a stronger position on moral equality than Kantian ethics. The focus on consistency is also a strength for persons who value respect for rationality. Finally, for some people, there is something compelling about acting from respect for the moral law. One problem with Kantian theory is related to the correct descriptions for actions and identifying the proper rules. Another main problem is how to resolve conflicting moral laws. These problems will prevent the ethical guidelines identified by the theory from being able to help us solve moral problems in many cases. Based on the criteria from Chapter 1, the Kantian ethical theory is only partially successful as an ethical theory. In the next chapter, we will look at another deontological theory, the moral rights ethical theory. This theory is similar to Kantian ethics in some ways but also has some important differences.

QUESTIONS FOR REVIEW

Here are some questions to help you review the main concepts in this chapter.

1. What are the basic ethical insights connected to Kantian ethical theory?

2. What additional ethical idea gives the theory its distinctive orientation? Does this idea have any appeal for you? Why, or why not?

3. What are the two formulations of the Kantian ethical standard or Categorical Imperative? Do you think that they are really saying the same thing, or do they have an important difference? Support your answer.

4. How are persons to know what personal rules they should will to be moral laws?

5. Identify one similarity and one difference between Kantian ethics and rule utilitarianism.

6. Identify one specific rule that Kantians would will to be a moral law and explain why they would do so.

7. How do Kantians justify their ethical standard?

8. How do Kantians differentiate between what is and what is not morally significant?

9. What position do Kantians take on the aspects of the traditional ethical assumptions?

10. What views does Kantian ethical theory take on each of the four ethical themes?

11. Identify one similarity and two differences between Kantian ethical theory and act utilitarianism?

12. What do you think is the most significant problem with Kantian ethical theory? Support your answer.

13. Is Kantian ethical theory a successful ethical theory based on the criteria from Chapter 1? Support your answer.

NOTES

1. A primary source for Kant's ideas on ethics is Immanuel Kant, *Groundwork of the Metaphysics of Morals,* translated by H. J. Paton (New York: Harper & Row, 1964).

2. One of this book's reviewers pointed out that even if we could obtain a legitimate ranking of moral laws this would not be sufficient. There might be cases where we would have a conflict between a very serious violation of a less important moral law and a minor violation of a more important law. The theory provides no direct guidance for resolving this kind of conflict.

Chapter 5

The Moral Rights Theory

Citizens of the United States are familiar with rights. The Declaration of Independence contains the idea that "all men" are endowed by God with certain "unalienable" rights and "that among these are the rights to life, liberty, and the pursuit of happiness." The U.S. Constitution also talks about rights in a number of areas, such as Article IX of the Bill of Rights, which says that "The enumeration in the Constitution, of certain rights, shall not be construed to deny or disparage others retained by the people." Americans are exposed to the language of rights almost constantly by media coverage of issues involving the civil rights of women, minorities, workers, and so on. International politics frequently focuses on moral rights violations, with arbitrary arrests of political dissidents and mass murders of ethnic minorities being common topics. We also encounter the language of rights in discussions of ethical problems such as abortion, affirmative action, euthanasia, and gun control. Because the language of rights is so prevalent, it is important to understand it better. In this chapter I will discuss an ethical theory centered on the idea of rights, the moral rights theory.

One major objection to act utilitarianism is that we should not sacrifice some persons for the good of others. This criticism relates to the idea that all persons are valuable as individuals. Act utilitarianism claims that the benefit of morally significant beings is of ultimate value and ought to be maximized. We might object, however, that it is not benefit or some state of affairs involving morally significant beings that is valuable, rather it is individual persons themselves. The ethical insight at the heart of the moral rights theory is that *individual persons are valuable and we should act in ways that respect their value.*

Who Has Moral Rights?

If persons are valuable, we ought to act in ways that respect their value. One way to respect the value of persons is to assert that they have *moral rights*. A common conception of moral rights is that they are legitimate claims to protection for certain basic interests or vital aspects of persons. (Another way to think about rights will be discussed later.) The British thinker John Locke (1632–1704) discussed natural rights, which he described as rights that God had given to some people. We might infer that Locke thought these natural rights had been given only to adult, white, male human beings because he did not oppose such things as slavery and the subordination of women and children. As the years have gone by, the idea of rights has changed in at least two ways. First, most proponents of moral rights no longer claim God as their source. They have proposed many ideas about the source of rights, grounding them in human nature, reason, or a social contract. Second, rights are no longer seen as being limited to adult, white, male human beings. Women, persons of color, and children are now included as persons having moral rights. There is also considerable discussion of rights for some nonhuman animals.

The concept of morally significant beings has been discussed in earlier chapters. I use the term "persons" to stand for "full-scale morally significant beings" who are entitled to the entire range of moral rights. There might also be second-class morally significant beings who are entitled to one or more moral rights, but not all of them. Proponents of animal rights sometimes argue that nonhuman animals are second-class morally significant beings possessing at least the right to life. This is argued especially for gorillas, chimpanzees, dogs, cats, cows, and dolphins, among others. To determine what beings count as persons we must employ a criterion or set of criteria. We will need another criterion or set of criteria to identify second-class morally significant beings—if we believe such a category exists. In Chapter 3 we encountered Bentham's idea that any being who could feel pain and pleasure should receive ethical consideration. If we use this criterion for persons, then these other mammals would definitely qualify.

In contrast, moral philosophers working on the problem of abortion have often argued for more demanding criteria for personhood. Mary Anne Warren argues that five traits are central to the concept of personhood: consciousness, reasoning, self-motivated activity, the capacity to communicate, and the presence of a self-concept and self-awareness.[1] Based on these criteria, most, if not all, nonhuman mammals would fail to qualify.

Determining the criteria for persons and second-class morally significant beings is an important matter. One possibility would be to use Warren's criteria as the standard for personhood and Bentham's criteria as the measure of second-class morally significant beings. However, the moral rights theory will work with any clear set of criteria, so the theory can be understood without resolving this difficult issue.

Moral Rights and Duties

John Locke claimed that there were three basic natural rights: the rights to life, liberty, and property. I prefer to call them moral rights and would add to this list, at least, rights to basic well-being and privacy, although some philosophers would argue that the first is packed into the right to life and the second into the rights to life and liberty. In 1948 the United Nations adopted the Universal Declaration of Human Rights (Appendix 2), which went far beyond Locke's basic three. Some of the rights included in this document are rights to work, education, and marriage.

When we think of moral rights as legitimate claims to protection, we are stating that to have a moral right to something is to be able to claim protection against other people violating or interfering with some vital interest. We claim such protection from other persons and from any institutions that have set themselves up as guarantors of moral rights, for example, governments. To have the right to life means that you are protected from other persons' killing you or taking your life. The essential idea is that persons are valuable, and we must protect their vital interests, such as life and liberty, using rights.

The idea of moral rights is correlated with the concept of duties. Moral rights impose duties on others. If I have a right to life, then other persons have a duty to respect my right to life and not to kill me. A rights-based theory promotes the impartial protection of vital interests. Any full-scale morally significant being or person has these rights and is protected regardless of intelligence, sex, race, or religion, and perhaps even without regard for species. The ethical standard identified by the moral rights theory is that *a person acts ethically if his or her action follows from one or more relevant rights and unethically if he or she violates another person's right or rights.* For example, if I steal your legitimately acquired television, I have violated your right to property and have acted unethically. Therefore, the initial claim is that your life, basic well-being, liberty, privacy, and property are protected; someone acts unethically when he or she violates your moral rights by depriving you of one or more of these things.

Basic Rights

Life

If the right to life is a protection right, it protects a person's existence, but it does not guarantee any particular quality of life. If someone has the right to life, you have a duty not to kill him or her, except in special cases. For example, if the only way you can defend yourself from someone killing you is to kill the person, you have not violated your ethical duty.

Although the right to life may seem clear and simple, it is not. Ethical issues such as abortion, suicide, euthanasia, and capital punishment raise questions about the right to life. We said that all persons have moral rights, but does the human embryo or fetus meet our criteria for a person? Do any nonhuman animals have the right to life? Is suicide unethical because it violates your own right to life? If a terminally ill person wants to die, does helping that person violate his or her right to life? Does the state act unethically when it legally executes someone because execution violates the criminal's right to life? These are a few of the interesting questions connected to the right to life.

Well-Being

If we limit the right to life to protecting life itself and do not extend it to protecting some degree of quality of life, then it is important to have a right to basic well-being. I would include both physical and psychological aspects of basic well-being in this analysis, although it will probably be much more difficult to identify cases where someone violates the psychological aspect of the right to basic well-being. Locke does not mention this right (perhaps because he thinks it is packed into the other basic rights), but I think including it clarifies matters. This right means that other persons have a duty not to treat a person in ways that would seriously harm the individual. The right to well-being is necessary because I may seriously injure someone without killing the person and violating his or her right to life. Persons should be protected from serious harm as well as loss of life. If I violate a person's right to basic well-being, I have acted unethically.

There are controversies connected to the right to basic well-being beyond the dispute over whether or not such a right exists. Some philosophers question whether a definitive line can be drawn between serious injury, which represents a violation of the right to well-being, and minor injury, which does not. Although I doubt that a definitive line can be drawn, we can surely identify some cases where there is serious injury and the right has indeed been violated. Another objection is that psychological injury should not be included. This objection is probably more practical than theoretical because we know that psychological injury can be as debilitating as physical injury. The concern is presumably not so much whether psychological injury can be serious but whether we can identify it. A related concern is whether we will be overwhelmed with violations of this right if it is included. Once again, although there may be cases where we cannot make a determination, there will be some cases where we can clearly see serious psychological injury. We need to consider such injury a violation of the right.

Liberty

The right to liberty protects our ability to make choices and decisions, to speak, to believe, to act to achieve our goals, and so on. The range of choices, beliefs, and actions protected is limited, however. The right to liberty protects ethical and legal choices and actions, not all choices or actions. For example, the right to liberty does not protect your ability to choose to go into a busy street and begin firing your gun at passing cars for target practice. This would be both unethical and illegal. We have a duty to respect the liberty of other persons as long as they exercise it in an ethical and legal manner. If a person prevents you from doing something you legally and morally ought to be able to do, your right to liberty has been violated.

The right to liberty probably generates more controversy than any other right. Although we can all agree that the right to liberty does not protect all actions, disagreements arise over exactly what should and should not be protected. We hear debates over the range of legitimate liberty in connection to issues such as freedom of speech, gun control, and (illegal) drug use. One guideline employed by moral rights proponents is that actions should be protected as long as they do not violate other basic rights. Other rights advocates worry about this strategy because it implies that other rights are more valuable than the right to liberty. When liberty comes in conflict with another basic right, liberty is the loser. More will be said about conflicting rights in a later section of this chapter.

Privacy

One way to interpret the right to privacy is to claim that it protects our control over information about and access to ourselves, but this control is limited by relationships.[2] When I enter into an employment relationship, I must give the employer certain personal information because it is necessary for the relationship. For example, I must provide data about my family if I want them to be covered by the company health plan.

I lose control over this information, relative to my employer, but the employer has not violated my right to privacy because this information was necessary for some aspect of the relationship.

In some cases acquiring knowledge about a person may not violate the person's privacy even if he or she does not wish you to have the information. Finding out from a third party that one's sexual partner has AIDS does not violate the partner's right to privacy. The nature of the relationship makes it necessary for the person to have this information. Disputes over the right to privacy arise when there is disagreement about whether information is necessary for a relationship. Some companies argue that they should know whether their employees use illegal drugs because this information is necessary for the employment relationship. Companies may institute drug-testing programs to gain this information even though the employees want to keep it secret. Drug testing does not distinguish between drug use on the job and on the employee's own time, and an employee who uses drugs only at home may test positive. Some employees claim that information about drug use away from work is not essential for the employment relationship and that obtaining such information through drug testing is a violation of privacy. Employers counter that information about any use of illegal drugs is relevant to the employment relationship, hence, there is no violation of privacy. This controversy illustrates the complicated nature of the right to privacy.

Property

The right to property protects our control over our property and our ability to gain the benefits of that property. Property, in one sense, means the tangible possessions we can legitimately own such as houses, land, cars, and televisions. In another sense property refers to intangible things such as original expressions of ideas and processes. My television is my property, but so is the song I composed. This control is limited by the power of a government to tax its citizens and legally take away some of their property. John Locke thought that governments should tax citizens only to gain funds for things that would benefit them directly; for example, government could tax citizens to build roads that they would use. Today, most philosophers interpret the power of government more broadly. Government can legitimately tax citizens for programs that only indirectly benefit them, such as foreign aid.

Similar to the other rights, there are controversies connected to the right to property. With a piece of property such as a television, we can use sales records to establish ownership. If the television is taken from the legitimate owner, the right to property has been violated. Property like computer software and videotapes of movies has made the concept of property more difficult for philosophers. A computer program can be copied from a friend's disk and the original remains with the friend. The software, in contrast to a television, can be used simultaneously by two people in different locations. Companies have tried to resolve this problem with respect to software by licensing consumers to use the software. The license is accompanied by one copy of the software and specifies the terms of the agreement; for example, the user may be permitted to use the software only on a single machine, or to make only one copy for a backup. Most software companies would argue that copying this kind of software is unethical as well as illegal. Issues like this one show that today the right to property is complicated and controversial.

An Alternative View of Moral Rights

Moral rights are usually seen as legitimate claims to protection for a basic interest, but they can also be viewed as ethical entitlements. Based on this alternative view, to have a right is to be entitled to the satisfaction of some interest. For example, the right to life does not merely protect you against others' taking your life but also entitles you to the minimum requirements necessary to sustain life. The contrast may be easier to understand if we discuss it in the context of the right to education mentioned in the United Nations Declaration of Human Rights. If there is a right to education and it is conceived as a protection right, the right protects us from other persons' denying us an education, assuming we have the financial resources and abilities to acquire one. If you have the money, the capabilities, and whatever else you need to attend school, your right to go to school is protected from the actions of other persons. You cannot be prevented from going to school because you are a woman, a minority group member, or for any other arbitrary reason. In the United States, however, the right to education is not merely a protected right. Here children are entitled to an education up to twelfth grade. If their parents cannot afford private school, children may attend public schools without paying tuition. Entitlement rights do not merely protect things we already have, they impose duties on the state to protect persons with those things. Social programs in the United States such as the Food Stamp program could be justified with entitlement rights. Persons are entitled to remain alive and in reasonable health. If they cannot secure enough property to sustain their lives and health on their own, the government must assist them.

Although we can construct reasonable arguments to include the rights to life, basic well-being, and property as entitlement rights, it is more difficult to interpret the rights to liberty and privacy as entitlement rights. It is difficult to see how persons could be provided with freedom or privacy; instead it seems adequate merely to protect persons from other persons' violating their freedom and privacy. Perhaps the most plausible option for those who want to see some rights as entitlement rights is to assert the existence of a mixture of rights, some being entitlement rights and others protection rights.

Justification and Determining the Morally Significant

Not all philosophers believe in moral rights. The utilitarian Jeremy Bentham thought that the idea of moral rights sounded important but that no such things existed. Philosophers and thinkers who believe in moral rights have offered many justifications for them. One simple justification is based on rationality and the idea that persons are valuable. If persons are valuable, then it would be irrational not to respect that value. One way to respect that value is to identify the important aspects of being a person and protect them. Thus, the ethical justification for moral rights is that they are a way to successfully protect the vital interests of persons, and it would be irrational not to protect these interests. This justification, like the justification for the Kantian ethical standard, ultimately rests on the idea that persons ought to be rational and that they ought to respect their rationality. As we saw in Chapter 4, there is no forceful reason why the capacity to be rational should require us to act from respect for that rationality. It is simply a basic premise of these two theories.

The moral rights theory claims that what is morally significant is what violates a moral right or what follows from a moral right. Things that have nothing to do with moral rights are not morally significant. This relationship to moral rights provides the differentiation between what is morally significant and what is not. If horses are not bearers of rights, then killing them is not morally significant unless doing so violates some right of persons (e.g., the right to property of the individual who owns the horses). Thus, the criteria for full-scale and second-class morally significant beings are crucial to what is and is not morally significant.

Moral Rights and the Traditional Ethical Assumptions

The moral rights theory accepts the traditional ethical assumptions. It would claim that ethics is rational because we can use reason to reach theoretical and practical conclusions about ethical matters. We can provide reasons to support our ethical guidelines and solutions to ethical problems; these reasons and solutions can be evaluated, and some can be evaluated as being better than others. For moral rights proponents, a compelling reason for judging an action to be unethical would be that the action violated some person's right. Proponents of moral rights would also agree that well-intentioned persons who share an ethical framework could discuss moral problems and arrive at mutually acceptable solutions. There is even some ground where advocates of moral rights can agree with proponents of competing ethical theories, especially Kantians.

Philosophers who accept moral rights endorse the view that all persons are moral equals. All persons have moral rights regardless of race, sex, religion, national origin, or intelligence (or possibly even species) and ought to receive the same ethical protection. For a believer in moral rights for all persons, there are situations in which to be ethical you must act contrary to your own self-interest. I might want to own a certain book that I cannot afford to buy. Perhaps you have this book, and I am certain I could steal it from you without being caught. Although it might be in my self-interest to steal the book, it would be unethical for me to do so because it would violate your right to property. I need to find some legitimate way to acquire the book or simply do without it so I do not violate any person's moral rights.

The moral rights theory also accepts the idea of universalizing ethical judgments. If a particular case is an example of violating a right and is unethical, then any sufficiently similar case is also unethical. It is unethical for me to steal your book, just as it is unethical for anyone else to do so. Regardless of what society or group the person belongs to, all persons have moral rights, and stealing violates the right to property in any society.

Moral Rights and the Basic Ethical Themes

The moral rights theory has a position regarding each of the four basic ethical themes discussed in Chapter 1. The first theme was represented by the question: Are some actions, beliefs, or values always either good or evil? Proponents of moral rights claim that some actions may be said to be objectively evil. Actions such as murder that violate one or more moral rights are objectively evil. Thus, certain classes of actions are objectively evil.

The second theme in ethics was indicated by the question: What makes something good or evil; is it the consequences that are produced or the reasoning that leads up to it? Advocates of moral rights focus on the reasoning that precedes an action. If I decide to steal your book because I want a copy of it but cannot afford to buy one, my action is unethical because I have not respected your right to property. I acted on self-interest with no consideration of your moral rights. Instead of thinking that the book was your property and that it would be wrong for me to steal it, I simply did what was in my own best interest. I did not respect your moral rights, therefore the action is unethical regardless of the consequences it might produce. It is possible that the consequences of the theft may produce a net benefit. For example, perhaps you did not really like the book and were not planning to reread it; I steal it, read it, and get a great deal of pleasure from it. The consequences would seem to be that you were not harmed and I was benefited; therefore the good consequence outweighed the bad. To a proponent of moral rights, the action is unethical no matter what the consequences may be. It is the lack of respect for your moral rights that matters, not the results of the action.

The third important theme related to the question: Should we faithfully follow general rules of behavior, or should we separately evaluate each action and belief? People who believe in moral rights claim that we can construct general rules that can function as ethical guidelines. "Killing innocent persons is evil" and "stealing another person's legitimate property is always unethical" are examples of moral rules or principles. If a class of action, like theft, always violates a moral right, then an ethical rule or principle can be constructed to articulate that insight.

The fourth theme is connected to the proper focus of ethical attention: Should the group, community, or majority of persons be the focus of ethics, or should the focus be on the individual? Advocates of moral rights assert that the focus of ethics should be the individual. Each person is protected by moral rights, and it is always unethical to violate that person's rights, even if doing so would benefit the group or the majority.

Contrasting Moral Rights with Act Utilitarianism

The moral rights theory and Kantian ethical theory are similar deontological theories (see Appendix 1), and comparing these two theories reveals few differences. A more interesting comparison would be between moral rights theory and act utilitarianism. Moral rights theory identifies acting from and violating moral rights as its main ethical guideline, whereas act utilitarianism relates good and evil to benefit and harm. Both the moral rights theory and act utilitarianism accept these aspects of the traditional ethical assumptions: that people are rational, that they are moral equals, and that they can universalize ethical evaluations. With respect to the four ethical themes, the theories agree on the first ethical theme, that some actions are objectively good and evil. They would, however, disagree on the remaining three ethical themes. They differ regarding how to evaluate good and evil. Act utilitarianism looks at consequences, whereas moral rights theory examines the reasoning that precedes an action. Another difference is that act utilitarianism evaluates acts separately, whereas moral rights theory endorses following general rules. Finally, utilitarianism concentrates on the greatest good for the greatest number of persons, whereas moral rights theory protects the individual person.

Problems with the Theory

The moral rights theory identifies ethical guidelines and argues that these guidelines are superior to those of other theories. The guidelines identified by the theory would clearly prevent the unlimited pursuit of self-interest. The problems with moral rights theory relate to the fourth criterion: that the theory must help us to solve ethical problems. I will discuss a few of the problems with the theory.

Descriptions of Actions

One problem related to the moral rights theory is that it, like Kantian ethics, seems to assume that there is only one accurate description of an action: an action either is theft and violates the right to property or is not theft and does not violate this right. Sometimes, however, there may be more than one competing description of an action. Suppose you want to avoid hurting Rose's feelings, and you tell her you admire her artwork when the truth is that you do not like it. Is the correct description of this action telling Rose a lie, complimenting Rose on her artwork, or trying not to hurt her feelings? If people do not agree on the description of the action, the moral rights theory cannot assess whether a particular right was relevant to the case. This problem relates to the fourth criterion for evaluating ethical theories. If we cannot fix the description of an action, we will not be able to identify the appropriate ethical guideline, in this case the relevant moral right. If we cannot identify the appropriate ethical guideline, we will not obtain help in solving the moral problem. Although this is a serious criticism, the theory would still work when there is agreement on the correct description of the action. This criticism shows that moral rights theory is only a partially successful ethical theory.

Conflicting Rights

Another criticism is that in cases where different rights come into conflict the theory can provide no adequate guidance to resolve these conflicts. This would also relate to the fourth criterion for evaluating ethical theories, that the theory must be able to help us solve moral problems. The abortion issue presents a prime example of this problem. Suppose a government that endorses moral rights is trying to create an abortion policy. If officials think the embryo or fetus qualifies as a person, then embryos and fetuses have the right to life. (They might also possess the right to life even if they only qualify as second-class morally significant beings.) Abortion kills the fetus and would violate its right to life. Thus, a policy allowing abortion would be unethical. The problem is that women have the right to liberty, and many people would argue that this right ought to protect a woman's ability to control what happens in and to her body. If women are to be able to control what happens in and to their bodies, they must be able to control their pregnancies. If they are to be able to control their pregnancies, they must be able to obtain abortions. A policy that would force a pregnant woman to give birth would seem to violate her right to liberty and would also be unethical. Therefore, we have conflicting rights, and it seems that any policy we make would be unethical.

This problem is similar to the problem of conflicting ethical rules that affects Kantian ethics. One way to begin to resolve this problem would be to create a legitimate ranking of the moral rights.[3] Assuming that the right to life outweighs the right to liberty, if the fetus is a bearer of moral rights, the anti-abortion policy is an ethical policy. However, no component of the theory seems to allow us to make such a ranking. The theory is designed to protect all of the vital aspects of persons. Intuitively, we usually regard life as more important than liberty. You do not have the freedom to shoot at cars passing by on the highway because the passengers' lives are more important than your freedom. In other cases, however, people seem to claim that liberty is more important. Many people assert that it is ethical for a person to commit suicide. Their position would seem to be that the person's right to liberty should protect the freedom to commit suicide, and outweigh the right to life. A skeptic might ask: Why is life more important than liberty? The skeptic's question may sound strange, but it points to the real problem. How can we argue that life is more important than liberty without appealing to consequences? If we start appealing to consequences, we will eventually turn into consequentialists and, probably, utilitarians. Think about a case where a man steals food from a wealthy family to feed his starving children. He could defend his action by saying that the children's right to life outweighed the rich persons' right to property, but this argument is just covert utilitarianism. There is more benefit in saving the children's lives, but maximizing benefit is not supposed to be the focal point of this theory.[4]

As the previous criticism shows, the moral rights theory has problems helping us solve some ethical problems. The theory will still work when there are no conflicting rights, and also in conflicts where we can reach compromise solutions that avoid violating either right. Proponents of the theory might insist that violating moral rights is always wrong and that we must search for solutions that resolve the conflicts without violating either party's rights. The potential thief must obtain charity or go on welfare to feed his starving children, and the pregnant woman ought to choose to give birth to her child and put it up for adoption. Opponents will probably say that such compromises are not always available in cases of conflict or that they may be unpleasant for those involved. Proponents of the moral rights theory would claim that such compromises are preferable to the more blatant violations of one of those rights. On the whole, this criticism implies that the theory will have only limited success.

The Community

The final criticism of moral rights theory does not relate directly to the criteria for evaluating ethical theories, but it might help someone compare act utilitarianism with moral rights theory. The criticism is that moral rights lead us to see persons as isolated, egoistic individuals who have no real identity with or obligations to a community, only minimal duties to other individuals. Karl Marx (1818–1883) states a variation of this criticism in his essay "On the Jewish Question":

> None of the supposed rights of man, therefore, go beyond the egoistic man... that is, an individual separated from the community, withdrawn into himself, wholly preoccupied with his private interest and acting in accordance with his private caprice.[5]

Marx interprets the right to liberty as the right to be separate from the community and the right to property as the right to act out of self-interest with regard to one's money and possessions. The right to property means that we have no obligation to use our property for the benefit of the community. The general criticism is that the moral rights view stresses individualism, self-interest, and egoism, and sacrifices the community. I believe that Marx exaggerates the extent of the egoism, self-interest, and isolation associated with moral rights theory, but it is correct that moral rights theory does not include obligations to the community as a whole, only obligations to individuals. Act utilitarianism operates for the benefit of the majority, and so produces obligations to benefit the majority of people in a community. This is an important difference between act utilitarianism and moral rights theory.

Conclusion

The moral rights theory and Kantian ethics are similar ethical theories. The moral rights theory has been included in this book because the language of moral rights is the most common ethical vocabulary in Western countries. Many people find moral rights more familiar, easier to understand, and more interesting than the various formulations of Kant's Categorical Imperative. Many contemporary ethical problems, such as abortion and euthanasia, are actually discussed by philosophers and nonphilosophers using the language of moral rights.

Moral rights theory originates from a reasonable ethical insight but ends up having problems with the descriptions of actions and with conflicting rights. Because of these problems, the theory will not always be able to help us solve ethical problems. The moral rights theory is a limited success as an ethical theory based on the criteria from Chapter 1.

The next chapter discusses a very different approach to ethics. Virtue ethics has a familiar ethical vocabulary (courage, generosity, justice, and so on), but it also has some ideas that are not so well known.

QUESTIONS FOR REVIEW

Here are some questions to help you review the main concepts in this chapter.

1. What is the ethical insight at the core of the moral rights theory?
2. What criteria would you use to determine status as a "person"? Do you think we need a category of second-class morally significant beings? If so, what criteria would you use for this class?
3. What are moral rights? According to John Locke, what are the three basic rights?
4. Identify three of the rights in the United Nations Universal Declaration of Rights (Appendix 2) that you regard as especially important. Explain why.
5. What is the ethical standard in the moral rights theory?
6. How does the right to well-being differ from the right to life? Should the right to well-being be included in the basic rights?

7. What is the right to privacy? How is it different from the right to liberty?

8. Explain the difference between rights as "legitimate claims to protection for basic interests" and rights as "entitlements." How would a proponent of each view interpret the right to an education?

9. Summarize the ethical justification for moral rights.

10. How do proponents of moral rights distinguish between what is morally significant and what is not?

11. How does moral rights theory incorporate the traditional ethical assumptions? Explain the moral rights position on each of the four ethical themes.

12. Discuss one similarity and two differences between moral rights theory and act utilitarianism.

13. What is the most serious problem with the moral rights ethical theory? Support your answer.

14. Why is moral rights theory only partially successful as an ethical theory?

NOTES

1. Mary Anne Warren, "On the Moral and Legal Status of Abortion," in *Morality in Practice,* edited by James P. Sterba (Belmont, CA: Wadsworth, 1997), p. 139.

2. I first encountered this definition of privacy in George Brenkert's article, "Privacy, Polygraphs, and Work," *Journal of Business and Professional Ethics,* Vol. 1, No. 1 (Fall 1981).

3. A rough intuitive ranking shows that we run into serious problems if we try to do this. Suppose we create the following ranking of some basic rights: (1) life, (2) well-being, (3) property, (4) privacy, and (5) liberty. Perhaps, however, property should come before well-being. We usually think it is wrong for people to steal even if they benefit by the theft. In freedom of speech cases, we sometimes allow people to say things that will harm others if the expressions are true. Does this mean that liberty is more important than well-being? These two examples already show that it would be difficult to create a ranking based on our intuitions. Some component of the theory is needed to order these rights, but there is no general agreement on this component.

4. One of the reviewers of this book pointed out that even if we could obtain a legitimate ranking of rights this would not be sufficient. There might be cases where we would have a conflict between a very serious violation of a less important right and a minor violation of a more important one. The theory provides no direct guidance for resolving such conflicts.

5. Karl Marx, "On the Jewish Question," in *The Marx-Engels Reader,* edited by Robert C. Tucker (New York: Norton, 1978), p. 43.

Chapter 6

Virtue Ethics

One way to determine good and bad is in relation to a goal, purpose, or function—something good helps accomplish the goal, promotes achieving the purpose, or helps carry out the function. If the primary function of my university is to educate students, then something that clearly promotes their education would be good relative to that function (e.g., skill in teaching because it promotes the education of students). If the university had a different primary goal, perhaps to maximize profit, different things would be good (e.g., skill in persuading students to pay higher tuition). The idea of good and bad being dependent on a goal, purpose, or function is often present in corporations, institutions, or organizations. Many corporations develop statements of their purpose and encourage employees to develop skills and techniques that will promote achieving that purpose. A purpose allows us to evaluate other things in relation to the purpose, but it does not allow us to assess the purpose itself.

This functional approach to good and evil can be applied to ethics in general. Aristotle uses it to develop a "virtue ethics" based on the distinctive function of human beings. If there is a such a basic function, then a good person is one who is successful at accomplishing it. Aristotle believes that the virtues are necessary for people to accomplish the basic human function and live good lives. The basic ethical insight associated with virtue ethics is that *the virtues help persons to achieve well-being or live good lives.* The additional ethical idea that makes Aristotle's virtue ethics distinctive is that there is a basic human function and that the virtues allow us to accomplish that function.

Virtue Ethics, Well-Being, and Reasoning

Virtue ethics, as presented in this chapter, is based on the ideas of the Greek philosopher Aristotle (384–322 B.C.E.). This ethical theory emphasizes being a good person instead of performing good actions and claims that the virtues are essential to being a good person. There are many possible definitions for "virtues," but the one used in this chapter must cover both intellectual and moral virtues. Therefore, *virtues* are character traits that promote the well-being of the person who has them.

Aristotle begins the *Nicomachean Ethics* with a discussion about the goals of human action.[1] He observes that the end, goal, or purpose for an action is always something that is good or which appears to be good. Some goals are means to achieve other ends and some are ends in themselves. Aristotle is interested in whether there is some ultimate end. Is there some goal or end that is not a means to anything else but is the ultimate end of all other goals? An answer to this question would have to reveal the ultimate end for all human beings, not just the ultimate end for some particular person. He suggests that most people call the ultimate end "eudaimonia," which might be translated as happiness, well-being, or flourishing. In this chapter, I will use "well-being." "Happiness" is the usual translation, but I believe it is misleading because it implies pleasure to many people. Aristotle believes that the ultimate end is a well-lived life, not a life filled merely with pleasure or happiness. The well-lived life includes not only pleasure and happiness, but also health, longevity, achievement, moral excellence, knowledge, wisdom, and other qualities. Therefore, the ultimate human purpose is well-being.

Aristotle is interested in what constitutes the well-being of humans as opposed to what makes up the well-being of other animals. He claims that human well-being is related to the basic or characteristic function of human beings. Just as a good flute player or sculptor is one who successfully fulfills the distinctive function of a flute player or sculptor, a good human being is one who successfully fulfills the characteristic function of a human being.

One of Aristotle's essential ideas is that there is a proper function for human beings. The human function is related to the capacity of humans that he thinks no other animal possesses—the ability to reason. If the distinctive function of human beings is reasoning, then human well-being or a well-lived life will be related to successfully fulfilling the function of reasoning well. It is not really necessary to limit this characteristic function to human beings, although Aristotle does so. If there are other beings who also possess reason as their basic function, then this form of well-being would be appropriate for them as well.

Intellectual Virtues

How does one reason well or successfully? First, reasoning well means being able to use reason to investigate things and to understand them. Aristotle claims that the proper end of this kind of reasoning is truth. This aspect of well-being is connected to what Aristotle labeled the intellectual virtues: scientific knowledge, excellence in art, practical wisdom, intuitive reason, and philosophic wisdom. Scientific knowledge deals with things that are unchanging or eternal where conclusions are arrived at by logic and observation. Excellence in art is concerned with making things. Practical wisdom involves deliberation about the means of achieving a good end, that is, making sound judgments about the conduct of life. It relates to discovering the appropriate actions to promote well-being as well as controlling the passion that might interfere with these appropriate actions. Intuitive wisdom is connected to understanding the first principles on which we base scientific knowledge. Finally, philosophic wisdom involves knowledge of the ultimate things. Part of well-being is reasoning well, and the intellectual virtues are connected to this. These virtues help persons to reason well.

In virtue ethics, the ethical standard will not be a rule or principle that designates ethical actions but rather *a moral model or ethical ideal of the virtuous person.* To be a virtuous person, the individual must strive to become more like the model. To begin to construct the moral model of a virtuous person, we might simplify Aristotle's intellectual virtues by claiming that there are only two of them: knowledge and practical wisdom. For contemporary people, this may seem to be an odd claim, but many ancient Greek philosophers believed that a knowledgeable person was living a better life than an ignorant one. Knowledge helps persons live better lives because knowledge opens up more opportunities and helps persons make better decisions. The virtuous person will be knowledgeable in a range of areas. Practical wisdom, the other intellectual aspect of the ideal ethical person, might be defined as the tendency or disposition to make sound judgments about the conduct of life. The virtuous person makes effective and fulfilling decisions and judgments and acts in appropriate ways. That person will also be able to live a better life. If we consider being knowledgeable and having practical wisdom as character traits, and if these traits can help us live better lives, then these traits fit the definition of virtues. They are character traits that promote the well-being of the person who has them.

Moral Virtues and Vices

Aristotle believes that virtue is connected to reasoning well. Therefore, to be virtuous we must not allow our emotions or passions to interfere with our reasoning. We sometimes see a situation where someone is too upset to think clearly; to reason well, we must avoid this. Aristotle claims that a person's emotional response is partly the result of teaching or training in accord with reason. People are taught to feel certain ways in certain situations. This produces habitual responses that are in accord with reason. Thus, a person's emotional response to a situation can be developed in accord with reason through teaching and can also be controlled by using reason.

Intellectual virtue is connected to knowledge and wisdom, but Aristotle claims that "moral virtue" is related to actions and the emotions or passions that accompany them. He states that an excess, a deficit, or an intermediate amount of emotion accompanies actions. An excess or a deficit amount of passion may interfere with acting rationally or ethically. Aristotle believes that the virtuous person feels a moderate amount of emotion in many situations and while performing many actions. An example of a virtue that involves moderation is courage. Courage involves feeling the right amount of fear and confidence when acting in dangerous or difficult situations. In battle, for example, the coward feels too much fear and not enough confidence, whereas the rash person feels too little fear and too much confidence. The coward runs away, and the rash person acts foolishly. Neither of these is the proper or rational action. Courage involves feeling a moderate amount of fear and confidence; this allows the person to act in a rational way. Aristotle calls the virtues connected to moderate emotional responses "moral virtues." The moral virtues also fit the definition of virtues as traits of character that promote the well-being of the person who has them. For example, courage is the disposition to feel the proper amount of fear and confidence in a dangerous or difficult situation, and this disposition promotes the person's well-being.

Moral virtues usually involve emotions and actions where excess and deficiency of emotion are wrong, whereas the virtuous action is accompanied by a moderate amount of emotion. This would lead us to conclude that the vices are always excesses or deficits of an emotion, but this is not true in all cases. Aristotle mentions vices such as spite, shamelessness,

SUMMARY OF SOME OF ARISTOTLE'S MORAL VIRTUES

Area	*Defect*	*Excess*	*Mean or Virtue*
Fear and confidence in dangerous situations	Cowardice	Recklessness	Courage
Desire for pleasure	Hardly ever found	Self-indulgence	Self-control (Temperance)
Giving and receiving money and things	Stinginess	Extravagance	Generosity
Getting angry	Apathy	Wrathfulness	Amiability
Telling the truth	Self-deprecation	Boastfulness	Truthfulness
Amusing others	Boorishness	Buffoonery	Wittiness
Pleasing others	Grouchiness or quarrelsomeness	Obsequiousness	Friendliness

and envy, and actions such as murder, theft, and adultery. These involve feelings that are evil in any amount (such as spite), and actions that are evil regardless of the feeling that accompanies them (such as murder).

Aristotle discusses a variety of other virtues that involve feeling the right amount of passion or emotion, although for modern readers some of the "emotions" may seem more like attitudes or orientations (see "Summary of Some of Aristotle's Moral Virtues"). I will mention only a few of the virtues he discusses. Moderation in regard to the passion involved with actions motivated by pleasure is self-control or temperance; excess is self-indulgence. Aristotle thinks a deficiency of the desire for pleasure is rarely found. In regard to the emotion connected to the action of giving and taking money or gifts, the mean is generosity, excess is extravagance, and the deficiency is stinginess. In connection with actions related to feelings of anger, people who feel the appropriate amount of anger are considered to be amiable. Those who feel too much anger are wrathful, and those who feel too little are apathetic. Aristotle also thinks a truthful person has found the mean between being boastful and being self-deprecating. A person who observes the mean in amusing others may be called witty. Someone who goes to excess is a buffoon, and someone who is deficient is humorless. In regard to the emotion related to actions connected to pleasing others, the virtue is friendliness, whereas excess is obsequiousness and a deficiency is related to quarrelsomeness or grouchiness. The important point is that in each of these virtues reason controls the amount of emotion a person feels and the moderation of emotion produces virtue.

Moral virtues are traits of character concerned with choice that involve moderation in action and emotion; this moderation is determined by a rational principle as discovered by a person of practical wisdom. Therefore, the intellectual virtue of practical reason and the moral virtues are closely related. The origin of action is choice, and the source of choice is desire and reasoning connected to achieving some goal or end. Virtuous action depends on practical wisdom guiding our choices and controlling our emotions.

It is difficult to reduce the ethical standard identified by Aristotle to a single phrase because it is composed of a number of aspects. A good person possesses the intellectual and moral virtues and does not have the vices. A good person is successful at using reason to understand the world and persons, is able to make sound judgments about the conduct of life, and does not allow excesses and deficiencies of emotion to interfere with reasoning well.

Aristotle claims that being a good person involves more than action. First, people must know what they are doing. This relates to the intellectual virtue, knowledge. Second, they must choose the action because it is virtuous and choose it as an end in itself. This relates to practical wisdom. Third, the action must be the expression of the character and must be accompanied by the proper feeling or emotion. This relates to moral virtue. Good people know what they are doing and choose to feel or do something because it is virtuous. Their feelings and actions flow from their character, and their emotions do not interfere with being virtuous. In addition, Aristotle thought that being a good person would only be possible in the presence of certain other factors, such as health, longevity, some degree of material prosperity, and living in a flourishing city. Without these things we would not really be able to live good lives.

Justification and Determining the Morally Significant

The ethical justification for using this standard connects to the assumption that there is a basic human function—reasoning—and that the well-lived life involves reasoning well. The justification for this ethical standard is that being a virtuous person will help us to accomplish the basic human function successfully.

It is difficult to know exactly how virtue ethics would separate the ethically significant from what is not ethically significant. Everything that promotes or detracts from well-being might be morally significant.

The well-lived life involves knowledge, practical wisdom, and feeling the right emotions, and also education, good habits, health, reasonable longevity, and so on. Thus, the range of the ethically significant is enormous.

Virtue Ethics and the Traditional Ethical Assumptions

Aristotle would probably disagree with most of what I have called the traditional ethical assumptions, but he would agree that ethics is rational. He would embrace the notion that persons can reach theoretical and practical conclusions about ethical matters. They can also provide reasons to support ethical guidelines and solutions to moral problems. These reasons and solutions can be evaluated, and some will prove to be better than others. He would also acknowledge that well-intentioned people who share a similar view of human well-being and the basic human function can discuss ethical problems and arrive at mutually acceptable solutions.

The question of moral equality is a difficult one for virtue ethics. Aristotle does not seem to have considered persons as moral equals. He endorsed slavery and believed that slaves could not achieve the same well-being as citizens as long as they were enslaved. Hence, they were not the moral equals of citizens. Does any version of virtue ethics have to reject moral equality? If an ethical person is one who is successful at fulfilling the basic function of rational beings (reasoning), then any rational being could, in theory, be ethical by being virtuous or reasoning well. One might argue that moral equality is consistent with this view because all persons have the same ethical starting point.

All human beings have a chance to strive for knowledge, practical wisdom, and moral virtue. Thus, in one sense, they are moral equals because they begin together. For Aristotle, however, reasoning well and being virtuous depend on opportunity and education. People (including slaves) who lack opportunities and who may be poorly educated will not be the moral equals of those who have more opportunities and are well educated unless they can develop virtuous habits through other means: acquiring informal education, emulating ethical persons, and so on. Aristotle would at least claim that it would be harder for slaves to live well than for citizens to do so. Although people may have the same theoretical starting point for ethics, as a practical matter some of them are hindered by their social positions. For Aristotle, people can also be morally disadvantaged by mental and physical factors. People who are seriously defective mentally will not have the same opportunities for knowledge and practical wisdom and hence will be hindered in achieving well-being. Similarly, neither will people who are seriously ill be able to achieve the full degree of well-being. Although Aristotle may endorse an original moral equality, it is soon outweighed by many practical ethical inequalities.

In a similar manner, it is difficult to reach a conclusion about universalizing moral judgments. Aristotle supported universal judgments about actions like adultery, theft, and murder. He probably would also have claimed that we can universalize judgments connected to the intellectual virtues. He would not have universalized judgments about the actions that flow from moral virtues, such as courage and generosity, and certainly not about what constitutes a moderate amount of emotion. He would claim that the mean with respect to emotion is not the same for everyone. With regard to Aristotle's ideas, we cannot always say that because an action is ethical for one person it must be ethical for anyone.

Virtue Ethics and the Four Ethical Themes

Relating virtue ethics to the four basic ethical themes is more difficult than doing so with the other theories. For the sake of comparison, however, I will try to do this. The first theme was represented by the question: Are some actions, beliefs, or values always either good or evil? Aristotle believes that some specific actions may be said to be objectively evil: murder, adultery, and theft. He also claims that certain vices are always evil: envy, shamelessness, and spite. Some virtues, such as practical wisdom, are always good. However, the moral virtues are not objective because the actual amount of emotion that constitutes the moderate amount varies from person to person. Even with this exception, however, there are some actions that are always good or evil.

Another significant theme in ethics was indicated by the question: What makes something good or evil; is it the consequences that are produced or the reasoning that leads up to it? Ethical action, with respect to the moral virtues, is primarily related to the proper amount of emotion, not to consequences or reasoning. Therefore, in one sense, this question is not really appropriate for Aristotle's ethics. The proper amount of emotion, however, is related to using reason to control the emotions and, therefore, we might say that moral action relates to reasoning. However, we might also say that virtue ethics is concerned with consequences. Ethical action is related to well-being, which is the ultimate goal of human virtue. All ethical actions are a means to achieve the ultimate end of well-being; hence, virtue ethics is also concerned with consequences. The answer, then, is that virtue ethics is concerned with both reasoning and consequences.

The third theme is related to the question: Should we faithfully follow general rules of behavior, or should we separately evaluate each action and belief? This question misses the point by an even wider margin than the previous one. Proponents of virtue ethics claim that people are not virtuous if they merely act virtuously. Virtuous action has several aspects. Virtuous people know what they are doing, they choose to do something because it is virtuous, and their feeling and actions flow from their character. The last part is crucial; ethical action flows from an ethical character, and an ethical character is a matter of good education and good habits. Ethical people do not need to follow general rules or evaluate individual actions because they have developed a good character and good habits. They act ethically in a spontaneous way, which is a product of character.

The fourth theme is connected to the proper focus of ethical attention: Should the group, community, or majority of persons be the focus of ethics, or should the focus be on the individual? Once again, it is difficult to answer definitively. The well-being that concerns Aristotle is the well-being of the individual. The goal of ethics is to discover the best life for an individual to live. Ethics, however, cannot be a matter of an individual acting in isolation. The virtuous person is necessarily social. He or she must live in a flourishing society and receive a proper education. Well-being cannot be achieved in isolation; it must be achieved together. Thus, virtue ethics includes both elements: individuals and the community. The goal of ethics is well-being for the individual, but well-being is necessarily social.

Differences Between Virtue Ethics and the Moral Rights Theory

Virtue ethics is radically different from the moral rights theory and other theories presented here (see Appendix 1). We find three major differences between virtue ethics and moral rights theory even before we look at the traditional ethical assumptions and the basic ethical themes.

The most important difference is the assumption by Aristotle that there is a distinctive human function. A second major difference is that virtue ethics is more interested in the person's character than in rights and actions. Aristotle's assumption is that good actions will flow from a person with a good character. Finally, virtue ethics connects the ethical life to factors like education, health, living in a flourishing state, and theoretical wisdom, which the proponents of the moral rights theory would say are not essential parts of ethics. Virtue ethics has a wider view of ethical life because it is involved with social, intellectual, and physical factors as well as with making decisions and acting.

Virtue ethics and the moral rights theory agree on two aspects of the traditional ethical assumptions. Both believe ethics is rational and that some moral judgments can be universalized. The theories differ, however, regarding whether people are moral equals. The moral rights theory clearly states that all human beings are moral equals and possess moral rights. Virtue ethics claims that people start out as moral equals but, as a practical matter, do not remain so.

In connection with the ethical themes, both ethical theories agree that some acts are always good or evil. The theories disagree on the other themes. The moral rights theory focuses on the reasoning that precedes action, but virtue ethics looks at both reasoning and consequences. The moral rights theory endorses not violating moral rights, a course that is similar to following rules. Virtue ethics does not center on either following general rules or evaluating actions. Finally, the moral rights theory concentrates on the individual, whereas virtue ethics is concerned equally with individuals and with groups.

Problems with Virtue Ethics

Lack of Effective Ethical Guidelines

Aristotle's ethical theory does identify moral guidelines and does argue that some ethical guidelines are better than others. It also identifies ethical guidelines that would prohibit the unlimited pursuit of self-interest. An important problem with the theory, however, is that the ethical guidelines it presents seem inadequate to really help us solve many moral problems. This point relates to criterion four: A successful ethical theory must help us to solve ethical problems. Aristotle provides only minimal guidelines about what actions should not be performed, for example, murder, theft, and adultery. Beyond these limited prohibitions, he offers little effective help. Discussion of the intellectual virtues does not help us to solve particular ethical problems. Knowledge is required to work out ethical problems, but knowledge alone is not enough to solve them. Practical wisdom is the tendency or disposition to make sound judgments about the conduct of life, and it would certainly lead to successful solutions to ethical problems. However, practical wisdom remains mysterious for Aristotle. The concept of practical wisdom is never extended to identify the solutions to ethical problems that would follow from practical wisdom.

The moral virtues provide no specific guidelines related to actions either. Aristotle presents the idea of a moderate amount of feeling, but the amount of feeling does not help us to solve moral problems concerning how we should act. Regardless of what we feel, we need help in knowing what to do. In addition, there is not even objective guidance about the proper amount of feeling as the mean is relative to the individual. Aristotle specifies no objective moderate amount of fear and confidence in dangerous and difficult situations that would produce an objective account of courage. In the case of an ethically significant choice, we might have several choices that could be accompanied by a moderate amount of emotion, and several moderate amounts of emotion that might accompany an ethical choice by different individuals. In general, Aristotle has not provided us with ethical guidelines that are adequate to help us solve many moral problems. Therefore, in light of its inability to completely satisfy criterion four, virtue ethics is not an entirely successful ethical theory.

Aristotle would not have viewed this lack of totally adequate ethical guidelines as a serious problem because he believed that good actions would necessarily flow from good character and that education was necessary for the development of good character. He thought that education would allow persons to develop the good habits needed to live well. If persons can live well as a result of possessing good habits, then they have no need for more precise ethical guidelines. This does not solve the problem, however, it only pushes it back one level. Aristotle has not provided educators with adequate ethical guidelines so that they would know how to educate the citizens to achieve good habits.

Moral Luck

A second problem concerns Aristotle's view that an ethical life contains a variety of components, some of which are beyond the moral agent's control. Well-being requires health, a reasonably long life, and living in a healthy society. None of these requirements is completely within the control of the agent. This produces a version of the problem of moral luck. If the well-being of the individual depends on these factors, then an element of luck enters the moral realm. It is a matter of luck whether I am born a healthy citizen in a flourishing society or a sickly slave in a society on the verge of collapse. Many philosophers would claim that the ability to be a good person should be completely in the control of the moral agent; virtue ethics is seriously flawed in this regard. This problem relates to the fourth criterion for evaluating ethical theories. If I live in an unsuccessful society, I will be less likely to develop a good character. If I do not develop a good character, I will be unable to solve ethical problems successfully. A successful ethical theory is supposed to help us solve moral problems, but Aristotle's theory cannot help us solve ethical problems if we have bad luck. We solve ethical problems successfully because we have good character, and good character depends on luck since many of the social, physical, and intellectual factors necessary to develop a good character are beyond the control of the individual.

The Fundamental Human Function

The final problem does not relate directly to any of the criteria for a successful moral theory, but it is probably the major reason people reject Aristotle's ethical theory. Aristotle argues that his ethical guidelines are the appropriate ones because they will help us to successfully accomplish the basic human function. He assumes the existence of a basic human function because of his assumption that everything has a basic function. However, Aristotle offers no compelling reasons to accept the position that everything has a basic function and that there is a distinctive human function. In the absence of such reasons, we are free to reject these ideas. If we reject the concept that there is a basic function for human beings, then we would also reject Aristotle's justification for choosing his ethical guidelines and his ethical guidelines.

Even if a person did accept the notion of a basic human function, he or she might not agree with Aristotle that the function was being rational. Aristotle claims that the basic human function must be related to whatever it is that only humans possess, and he thinks that humans alone are rational. Therefore, the human function is rationality. A couple of problems surface in regard to this. First, rationality might not be the exclusive possession of human beings. Our conclusion depends on how rationality is defined. Perhaps a gorilla who can learn to use sign language is rational. If rationality is not an exclusively human possession, then Aristotle's reason for choosing it is based on a mistake. Another problem is that the basic human function might not be related to something only humans possess; perhaps humans share their basic function with other species. It has been suggested that the fundamental human function, like that of any living organism, is to reproduce and pass on its genetic code. If our basic function is shared with other species, then Aristotle's decision to base ethics on our exclusive, basic function is mistaken because humans have no exclusive, basic function. Finally, even if the basic function is an exclusive human possession, that function might not be being rational. Some Christians believe that the fundamental human purpose is to love God and other human beings. We might argue, using Aristotle's reasoning, that because only human beings can love God and other human beings, the basic human function is to do so. There are many reasons to reject the most basic part of Aristotle's ethical theory, and subsequently, his ethical guidelines.

Conclusion

Although virtue ethics begins with an interesting insight, it ends with problems. The theory's strength is that it clearly expands beyond ethical rules and actions the morally significant aspects of being a person. It is also interesting because it illustrates the functional approach to ethics. One of its main weaknesses is the absence of a convincing justification for the notion of a basic human function that should ground ethical guidelines. This lack of justification illustrates a crucial problem for all functionalist ethical approaches—the justification of the purpose or function is typically the weakest part of the theory. Because the theory evaluates everything in terms of the function, it has trouble evaluating the purpose or function itself. Another major problem is that the ethical guidelines are inadequate to help us solve many ethical problems. Based on the criteria in Chapter 1, Aristotle's virtue ethics would not be a completely successful ethical theory. Next I will turn to the final approach to ethics, the ethic of care.

QUESTIONS FOR REVIEW

Here are some questions to help you review the main concepts in this chapter.

1. What is the ethical insight associated with virtue ethics? What additional idea helps make Aristotle's version of virtue ethics distinctive?
2. What, in general, are virtues?
3. In Aristotle's opinion, what is the distinctive function of human beings?
4. What are the intellectual virtues? How do they help persons achieve well-being?
5. What are the moral virtues? Provide a detailed explanation of Aristotle's account of courage to illustrate a moral virtue. How would courage help persons to achieve well-being?
6. What is the ethical standard for virtue ethics? What is the justification for using that standard?
7. Would virtue ethics endorse aspects of the traditional ethical assumptions?

8. What position would virtue ethics take on each of the four ethical themes?

9. Identify three major differences between virtue ethics and moral rights theory.

10. Which problem with virtue ethics do you think is the most serious? Explain why.

11. Would virtue ethics be a successful ethical theory based on the criteria in Chapter 1? Explain why, or why not.

12. Do you believe there is a basic human function shared by all people? If so, what is it?

13. What is character? How would you describe your character? If you wanted to improve your character, how would you go about doing so? How would you know that you were headed in the right direction?

NOTES

1. Aristotle, *Nicomachean Ethics,* translated by J. A. K. Thomson (London: Allen & Unwin, 1953).

Chapter 7

The Ethic of Care

The final ethical theory to be discussed is the ethic of care. This is a contemporary ethical theory, and I will begin by summarizing the key ideas developed by Nel Noddings in her book, *Caring: A Feminine Approach to Ethics and Moral Education.*[1] Noddings presents the ethic of care as an alternative to traditional ethical theories. She believes that ethical behavior is connected to human emotional response and the interdependence of people. Therefore, her ethic focuses not on reason and ethical principles but on using ethical caring as the model of an ethical relation.

The Background to Noddings's Theory

Noddings's ideas about caring can be understood in the context of the work of two psychologists, Lawrence Kohlberg and Carol Gilligan. Kohlberg concluded from his research that all human moral development follows a necessary path through three levels, although many people do not progress all the way.[2] At the first level good and bad are understood in relation to power, reward, and punishment; at the second level good and bad are related to the moral guidelines of groups and society. Finally, at the highest level people view ethics in terms of objective moral principles. The highest stage for Kohlberg is centered on justice, and among the theories in this book, Kantian ethics would best represent this highest stage.

Carol Gilligan agrees with Kohlberg that there are levels of moral development; she believes, however, that Kohlberg's levels represent a view of moral development centered around justice, which does not explain the moral development of all human beings. She claims (or originally claimed) that this is a masculine way of talking about ethics and suggests that this masculine character may have originated from the fact that Kohlberg used only males in his original studies. She also notes that women often failed to achieve the highest moral stage in Kohlberg's hierarchy.

Gilligan's research suggests a different way of talking about ethics, one more involved with relationships, care, and nonviolence than with justice. The title of her influential book, *In a Different Voice,* highlights the idea that there is an alternative way to talk about ethics.[3] She points out that it is mostly women who employ this different way of discussing ethical problems. Like Kohlberg, Gilligan claims that there are three levels to moral development. At the first level the person is oriented toward individual survival; at the second level goodness is understood in terms of self-sacrifice. At the third level nonviolence or the injunction against hurting others is elevated to a principle governing everyone, the moral agent as well as others affected by her actions. It is on this level that care becomes a universal obligation.

For many moral philosophers, and even some psychologists, the Kohlberg/Gilligan theory of progressive moral levels is problematic. As psychologist Norma Hahn points out, these researchers claim to be merely describing the moral development of human beings, but by ranking the various moral orientations, they are inserting their own ethical judgments about what is better and what is worse. She states that researchers cannot rank moral thinking without taking a normative moral position, whether they know it or not.[4]

Kohlberg places justice at the top because he assumes (perhaps unknowingly) that it is the closest to a legitimate moral theory. He does not reveal the objective criterion or set of criteria he used to rank these approaches to good and evil, nor why this criterion or set of criteria is the best one.

Gilligan's approach reveals the same problem. She ranks the nonviolent orientation at the highest level because it fits her normative position. Like Kohlberg, she is not clear about the criterion or set of criteria grounding the ranking, nor why that set is better than any alternatives. Psychologists can certainly identify different ways of talking about good and bad that people actually employ, but they should be careful about ranking these different moral languages. Clear evaluative criteria are needed to produce legitimate rankings, and the psychologists need to explain what their criteria are and why their criteria are the best ones to use.

Nel Noddings's ideas are more appropriate for a discussion of ethics than either Kohlberg's or Gilligan's because she does not suggest that moral development moves through a necessary hierarchy. Noddings does, however, retain the idea that there are masculine and feminine ways of discussing ethics. She also retains Gilligan's interest in nonviolence and caring. Noddings develops an ethic of care that can be traced back to Gilligan's rejection of the justice approach as the best way of discussing ethics.

Natural and Ethical Caring

Most of us have been cared for by a person or persons, if only our parents. We value the memories of being cared for and the relationship of care. The ethical insight of the ethic of care is that *ethics is primarily concerned with relationships between persons.* The additional idea essential to developing an ethic of care is that the ultimate relationship, in an ethical sense, is caring.

Nel Noddings claims that human encounter and emotional response are basic aspects of human existence. People are necessarily interdependent and are the products of the various relationships in which they are involved. Ethical action arises out of these relationships, not out of isolated individuals following moral rules. She identifies natural caring—the relation in which we care for another out of love or natural inclination—as the human condition that is consciously or unconsciously perceived to be good. Ethical caring—the relation in which a person meets another morally—arises out of natural caring. Noddings asserts that ethical caring can be used as a moral model.

Ethical caring requires that the one who cares for the other (the one-caring) must try to apprehend the other's reality. The one-caring must consider the other's nature, way of life, needs, and desires. Ethical caring involves engrossment; the one-caring is concerned with the cared-for, is present in his or her acts of caring, and tries to feel what the other is feeling. Motivational displacement is another part of ethical caring: The one-caring is motivated by the good of the other (the cared-for). There is a displacement of interest from his or her own reality to the reality of the cared-for. Finally, the one-caring is directed toward the welfare, protection, and enhancement of the cared-for. An ongoing caring relationship requires a commitment on the part of the one-caring to act for the benefit of the cared-for. On the other side of the relation, the one who is cared for must recognize that the one-caring cares for him or her. Noddings concludes that, "One must meet the other as one-caring. From this requirement there is no escape for one who would be moral."[5]

According to Noddings, ethical caring depends on two sentiments and on memories of caring and being cared for. First is the "sentiment of natural caring."[6] She describes this sentiment as the "natural sympathy that human beings feel for each other."[7] Second is the sentiment that arises when we remember our best experiences of being cared for and caring for others. This sentiment is characterized as a "longing to maintain, recapture, or enhance our most caring and tender moments."[8] This second ethical sentiment produces an "I must" or moral obligation in response to the plight of the other. It arises from our evaluation of the caring relation as being superior to other forms of relatedness. We long to be in caring relationships, and that longing provides a major motivation for us to care for others and to be moral. Noddings also claims that we have memories of those times when we were cared for and in which we cared for others, and that we can choose to use these memories to guide our conduct. The memories and sentiments are associated with the ethical ideal.

Ethical Obligation and the Ethical Ideal

When I reflect on the way I am in genuine caring relationships, Noddings thinks that I form a picture of myself. This picture of myself as cared-for and one-caring is accompanied by an awareness of the goodness of natural caring. In connection with this picture and awareness, I form an ideal picture of myself as one-caring and cared-for. When I am confronted with the plight of a potential cared-for, I feel compelled to respond because I realize that caring or not caring will enhance or diminish the ethical ideal. I feel that I must do something. The motivational power of this "I must" is related to the value I place on moving toward my ideal picture of myself and on the importance of the relationship of caring. If I want to be ethical, I am obligated to meet the other as one-caring, to increase my virtue as one-caring, and to enhance my ethical ideal. This ethical obligation depends on the existence of or potential for a close relationship with the person and "the dynamic potential for growth in relation, including the potential for increased reciprocity and, perhaps, mutuality."[9] The potential for an effective caring relationship helps to determine whether there is an obligation, and the chance of reciprocity helps us to prioritize our obligations. The greater the potential for a reciprocal relationship of caring, the higher a priority I should give to developing the relationship.

The Ethical Standard of the Ethic of Care

Noddings claims that we form an ideal picture of ourselves as one-caring and cared-for. We realize that caring or not caring will enhance or diminish the ideal picture. This picture of an ideal caring self can act as a moral model, ethical ideal, or ethical standard. *Anything that moves the person closer to being more like the ethical ideal will be good; anything that moves the person farther away from being like the ethical ideal will be bad.* In relation to the ethical ideal, caring is good, whereas violence or hurting others is almost always bad.

We ought to be cautious about this ethical standard, however. Noddings states that her primary focus is not on good and bad but on moral perception and sensitivity, although she does acknowledge that good and bad are useful concepts. The one-caring, she asserts, can make judgments of good and bad by basing them on whether the thing being judged promotes or inhibits caring. For example, hurting people is usually wrong because it inhibits caring for people and detracts from the ethical ideal. Unless I act out of self-defense, hurting some people does not help me to better care for others. She seems to think that I need to examine situations and strive to find ways to care for people without hurting others. I determine right and wrong in relation to my ideal picture of myself as one-caring and cared-for. This picture has objective elements based on my experiences with effective caring; that is, some things have promoted effective caring and others have not. These objective elements related to my actual experiences with caring help prevent the ethic of care from becoming a form of ethical subjectivism.

The Limit of Ethical Caring and the Morally Significant

Noddings denies that we are obligated to care for everyone. Relationships determine the nature of ethical obligation. We should care for those with whom we already have a caring relation or with whom there is potential for an effective caring relation. The relation or the potential for an effective caring relation helps establish the limits of obligation. The greater the potential for an effective and reciprocal caring relation, the higher a priority I should give to developing it. We do not have to feel obligated to care for those who are distant and with whom we have no real potential for an effective caring relation unless we abandon already existing caring relations. One metaphor she uses is that of concentric circles; we care most for those in the inner circles, and less as the circles become more distant. She illustrates the point with this example: "I am not obliged to care for starving children in Africa, because there is no way for this caring to be completed in the other unless I abandon the caring to which I am obligated."[10] We may still choose to do something for these children, but we are not obligated to do so. The limit of our obligation is based more on the potential for effective caring and existing caring relationships than on geography. My grown child may move to Africa, but I am still obligated to care for him or her to the best of my ability. Of course, geography makes it much harder to develop caring relationships; it is much easier for me to develop a relationship with the children living in poverty next door than with the impoverished children living in Africa.

Another limitation to the obligation to care is connected to the idea that the one-caring must also protect him- or herself from abusive or harmful relationships that would interfere with the ability to care for others. We are not obligated to care for people who threaten our ability to care for others or ourselves. Those who care must care for themselves as well as others, and they must limit their caring so that they can maintain themselves and their ability to care in the future.

The limits of effective caring would seem to differentiate between what is and is not morally significant, at least in the strongest sense of the morally significant wherein we are obligated to respond to that significance. Things that relate to those we care for are the most morally significant for us, and our moral obligations relate to these relationships of care.

Justification for the Ethical Standard

The ethic of care strives to promote the attitude of caring. It is centered on each person's ethical ideal, the ideal picture of oneself as cared-for and one-caring. This ethical ideal motivates us to enter into caring relationships because we know that caring or not caring will move us closer to or farther away from our ethical ideal, and our desire is to move closer to it. The justification for the ethical standard is, presumably, that we value moving closer to our ideal pictures of ourselves as one-caring and cared-for because we know ethical caring is good. We know that ethical caring is good because it is modeled on natural caring, and we intuitively know that natural caring is good. Knowing intuitively that natural caring is good, we ought to engage in natural caring and also in the ethical caring that is modeled on it. This makes the justification ultimately rather mysterious because it depends on an intuition about natural caring. The intuition does, however, present a nice contrast to Kantian ethics. If you are driven by a respect for rationality, you might become a Kantian; whereas if you are inspired by the intuition that natural caring is good, you might adopt the ethic of care.

The ethic of care is centered around the ideal picture of ourselves as one-caring and cared-for. Good and bad relate to our moving closer to the ideal or farther away from it. Our ethical obligations arise from our longing to be in caring relations and our intuition that natural caring is good. We must meet people, within certain limitations, as one-caring to maintain the ethical ideal. The ethic works by examining particular cases in light of the caring relation. It emphasizes moral perception and sensitivity and acting as one-caring in our various human relationships.

The Ethic of Care and
the Traditional Ethical Assumptions

Nel Noddings would reject what I have called the traditional ethical assumptions. She believes that ethics is based primarily on sentiment, not reason. Moral obligation relates primarily to the two sentiments discussed earlier and to the value we place on our ideal picture of ourselves as caring individuals, not to rational arguments. She does not, however, dismiss reason completely. Noddings would agree that we could provide reasons for our ethical evaluations, for example, that stealing from someone does not enhance a person's ethical ideal as one-caring. She would also acknowledge that well-intentioned people who share a similar view of caring could discuss moral problems and arrive at mutually acceptable solutions.

Noddings does not endorse moral equality. We are morally obligated to care for those closest to us but are not obligated to care for children in foreign countries. People are not moral equals; the degree to which we should care for them relates to our relationships with them and the potential for developing and maintaining effective caring relationships.

Noddings also rejects the idea of universalizing moral judgments. Each case needs to be examined in the light of caring. She wants to preserve the uniqueness of human encounters. Claiming that subjective experience is essential to ethical encounters, Noddings asserts that conditions are seldom sufficiently similar for one moral agent to declare that everyone who wants to be ethical must perform or not perform this action. She does, however, insist that there is universal access to the caring attitude.

The Ethic of Care and the Four Ethical Themes

The first ethical theme is related to the question: Are some actions, beliefs, or values always either good or evil? Noddings believes that everyone consciously or unconsciously perceives the relation of natural caring as good. This probably leads to actions that are objectively good, but such actions would have to be beneficial to the cared-for and not be harmful to the one-caring. For example, it is always good for a person to care for a seriously ill family member when this caring does not harm the one-caring. Noddings is hesitant, however, about this matter; she wants to preserve the subjective aspect of human encounter and examine each ethically significant case separately.

The second ethical theme is indicated by the question: What makes something good or evil; is it the consequences that are produced or the reasoning that leads up to it? It seems to me that Noddings is more concerned with consequences. The one-caring must act for the benefit of the cared-for, and this means that consequences are essential. If my caring does not benefit the cared-for, then I have not acted ethically. However, reasoning is also connected to ethical action. The one-caring must try to understand the other's situation, nature, way of life, needs, and desires to discover how best to care for the person. Discovering how to best care for the person will certainly embody reasoning. To be ethical, my action must benefit the cared-for and must also flow from my understanding of his or her reality and my reasoning about how best to care for that person. The ethic of care involves both reasoning and consequences, but because the reasoning is directed toward enhancing the welfare of the person cared-for the main focus is on consequences.

The third theme is connected to the question: Should we faithfully follow general rules of behavior, or should we separately evaluate each action and belief? Noddings rejects general rules and argues that we must examine each case to see what is best for the one-caring to do.

The fourth theme is related to the proper focus of ethical attention: Should the group, community, or majority of people be the focus of ethics, or should the focus be on the individual? Noddings believes that we must focus on the individual cared-for. We must relate to people as unique individuals, and we must preserve the "subjective aspect" of human encounter.

Some Differences Between the Ethic of Care and Virtue Ethics

Noddings's ethic of care is an interesting addition to the ethical conversation and reveals some important differences from virtue ethics and the other ethical theories (see Appendix 1). The ethic of care and virtue ethics are in agreement on two points. Both theories reject moral equality. They also maintain that some actions are objectively good or evil.

One of the main differences between the ethic of care and virtue ethics is that Noddings's theory does not endorse the idea of a basic purpose shared by all human beings. The ethic of care is also much less based on reason. It grounds ethics in sentiments, memories, and an ideal relationship, not in reasoning successfully. Virtue ethics does include sentiment as morally significant but is concerned primarily with moderating sentiment, whereas Noddings endorses the two sentiments connected to ethical caring. The two theories also disagree on universalizing some moral judgments. Noddings is strongly against universalizing moral judgments.

The two ethical theories disagree on three of the four basic ethical themes, accepting only objective good and evil. Virtue ethics is not focused on rules or actions and is concerned with both the group and the individual. The ethic of care centers on actions and individuals. Virtue ethics relates good and evil to both reasoning and consequences. The ethic of care connects good and evil mainly to consequences. Because of these important differences, the two ethical theories offer contrasting approaches to ethics.

Problems with the Ethic of Care

The ethic of care does identify some ethical guidelines and argues that they are better than some other possible guidelines. It clearly identifies ethical guidelines that would prohibit the unlimited pursuit of self-interest. It does, however, develop some problems related to the fourth criterion: The theory must be able to help us solve ethical problems.

The ethic of care is a contemporary theory, and I will look at another contemporary source to identify some of the main problems with the theory. One of the best of the numerous discussions of Noddings's views is found in Claudia Card's article, "Caring and Evil."[11] Her main question is: "Can an ethic of care without justice enable us adequately to resist evil?"[12] Card identifies problem areas that would seem to indicate a negative answer to this question.

Incomplete Moral Standard

The first problem area involves the evils that strangers inflict on strangers. Card states that "resting all of ethics on caring threatens to exclude as ethically insignificant our relationships with most people in the world, because we do not know them individually and never will."[13] No one has the responsibility to care for everyone in the sense of "caring" central to the ethic of care: We do not have the moral obligation to care for Africa's starving children. The implication of this argument is that Noddings has given us no guidance about how to avoid acting unethically in regard to most of the people in the world, people whose lives we may affect for the worse even though we have no personal relationship with them. Card claims that because we cannot have caring relationships with most of the people in the world, we need other grounds for moral obligations toward them, such as justice. Thus, she believes that the ethic of care is incomplete. This criticism relates to the fourth criterion for evaluating ethical theories: The theory must help us to solve ethical problems. If the ethic of care is incomplete and does not provide moral guidelines that relate to most of the world's people, it will not help us to solve ethical problems connected to these people. Therefore, it will only partially satisfy criterion four.

Exploitation of the One-Caring

The second problem area involves the evil that intimates do to each other. According to Card, if we use caring as a base for ethics, we are "in danger of valorizing relationships that are sheerly exploitative of our distinctly human capacity to take another's point of view."[14] Card is claiming that the ethic of care might endorse relationships where people who are required to take the other's point of view are valued simply for what they contribute to others or the projects of others, instead of being valued for themselves, as persons with their own ends and projects. Her point is that maintaining the extreme value of caring relationships in all cases will lead to the one-caring being exploited or taken advantage of by the cared-for. Because Noddings claims that if we must exclude someone from our caring we act under a diminished ethical ideal, there is ethical pressure to maintain exploitative relationships that perhaps ought to be dissolved. Card observes that there are some caring relationships from which the one-caring ought to be able to withdraw without being "ethically diminished." We must be able to withdraw from exploitative or abusive relationships with intimate partners or family members without diminishing the ethical ideal. Card points out that caring has the consequence of supporting people's projects, and that caring, unrestrained by other values, might lead us to support immoral projects. She claims that "[i]t is better to cease caring than to allow one's caring to be exploited in the service of immoral ends."[15] Once again, Card has identified an area where she thinks the ethic of care is incomplete.

Caring needs to be supplemented with other moral values, such as justice, so that the one-caring can evaluate his or her caring relations and withdraw from those that are supporting unethical projects or exploitation. This criticism also relates to criterion four. If the ethical guidelines identified by the ethic of care are incomplete, then the theory will not be adequate to help us solve all moral problems. The one-caring will not be able to solve all the moral problems connected to caring, unless there is some additional ethical standard to allow the one-caring to identify unethical projects and instances of exploitation and to determine what will really promote the welfare of those involved.

Limits on Promoting Welfare

The final problem concerns one of my own questions about the ethic of care? Why is ethical caring, which limits promoting the welfare of others to a relatively small group of people, preferable to maximizing the welfare of the greatest number of people? We might begin to think about this by asking, Why is ethical caring good? Ultimately the goodness of ethical caring seems to be grounded in the claim that all humans consciously or unconsciously perceive natural caring to be good. This thesis is a factual hypothesis and could be supported with research of the type done by Kohlberg or Gilligan. Noddings, however, offers no empirical evidence for this claim. Of course, even if people do perceive natural caring as good, it does not mean that they ought to do so. To strengthen this theory, Noddings needs an argument to support the claim that we ought to perceive natural caring as good. She then needs another argument establishing a tighter connection between natural and ethical caring, or a separate argument to show why ethical caring is good.

Natural caring is illustrated by a parent's caring for a helpless infant. Natural caring is vital to the survival of the species because human beings are born helpless and must be cared for to survive. If we believe that the survival of particular human beings and of the species in general is good, then natural caring is a good means to help accomplish these ends. Ethical caring, however, is not always related to survival. It is related to the well-being of the other, which extends beyond survival. Why is it good to promote the well-being or benefit of others? Utilitarians have one kind of answer to this question, but it is a response associated with benefit being the ultimate end of action and the ultimate good. If benefit is the ultimate good, then we should try to maximize it for as many people as possible. Noddings thinks we should promote the welfare or benefit of those with whom we have developed relationships of care, but why limit it to these people? Perhaps her answer would be that limiting the number of people whose welfare we promote will make us more effective at helping others. She might believe that utilitarianism is ineffective because the ethical concern is spread out over all morally significant beings, whereas the ethic of care is more effective because it concentrates the ethical focus. Would the ethic of care be more effective, and is effectiveness a sufficient justification to choose an ethical theory?

Conclusion

The idea that an ethic could be based on care generated a considerable amount of interest among moral philosophers. Most moral philosophers, however, still seem more comfortable with an ethics based on rules and principles rather than an ethics based on relationships and care. In spite of the problems with this theory, the ethic of care is an interesting addition to the ethical conversation. The strength of this theory is that it allows special treatment for those who are closest to us, without this special treatment being unethical. Most ethical theories emphasize moral equality and cannot respond to the special relationships that we have with friends and family members. The theory does seem to be incomplete, however, and therefore it will not always be successful in helping us to solve moral problems.

I have briefly examined six ethical theories and found that there are problems with all of them. In the final chapter I discuss the possibility that a pluralistic ethics can do a better job of solving moral problems and helping us live together successfully than can any single ethical theory.

QUESTIONS FOR REVIEW

Here are some questions to help you review the main concepts in this chapter.

1. According to Noddings, what is natural caring?
2. What are the key elements of ethical caring?
3. What are the two sentiments essential to ethical caring? Why are they essential?
4. What is the ethical ideal, and how do we enhance it or detract from it?
5. How does a person make judgments about right and wrong based on the ethic of care?
6. Does the ethic of care accept the traditional ethical assumptions? Support your answer.
7. How does the ethic of care relate to the four ethical themes?
8. What are two differences between the ethic of care and most of the other ethical theories we have discussed?
9. Which problem with the ethic of care seems most serious to you? Explain why. Why would the ethic of care not always be successful in helping us solve ethical problems?

10. Do you think there are distinctively masculine and feminine approaches to ethics? Support your answer.

NOTES

1. Nel Noddings, *Caring: A Feminine Approach to Ethics and Moral Education* (Berkeley: University of California Press, 1984).

2. Lawrence Kohlberg, "Moral Stages and Moralization: The Cognitive-Development Approach" in *Moral Development and Behavior,* edited by T. Lickona (New York: Holt, Rinehart and Winston, 1976). Each of Kohlberg's levels has two stages. To simplify things, I have merely tried to summarize the levels.

3. Carol Gilligan, *In a Different Voice: Psychological Theory and Women's Development* (Cambridge: Harvard University Press, 1982).

4. Norma Haan, "Can Research on Morality Be Scientific?" *American Psychologist,* October 1982, 37(10): 1096–1104.

5. Noddings, *Caring: A Feminine Approach to Ethics and Moral Education,* p. 201.

6. Ibid., p. 79.

7. Ibid., p. 104.

8. Ibid.

9. Ibid., p. 86.

10. Ibid.

11. Claudia Card, "Caring and Evil," *Hypatia,* 1990, 15(1): 10.

12. Ibid., p. 101.

13. Ibid., p. 102.

14. Ibid.

15. Ibid.

Chapter 8

A Pluralistic View of Ethics

In Chapter 1, I claimed that the most important function of ethical theories is to identify moral guidelines that can help us live together successfully and solve ethical problems. None of the theories discussed in this book is able to accomplish that function with complete success. Because there are problems with all the theories, you may conclude that learning about ethical theories is a waste of time. I think this conclusion is a mistake. This final chapter is a simple sketch of a way of thinking about ethics and ethical theories, and I encourage you to try to fill it out for yourself. There are problems with ethical theories, but I believe that we have to work with what we have and make the best of it.

The key to understanding the value of ethical theories is to see them as tools to help us live together successfully and solve moral problems. Like our familiar hand tools, each one is best at helping us accomplish a certain job, and none of them is appropriate for every job. A hammer is useful for driving nails, but if you need to tighten a bolt, you should use a wrench. Living together successfully and solving moral problems may seem like one "job" that can be accomplished by one theory, but I believe living together successfully and solving moral problems involves many jobs. We need more than one theory (or tool) to accomplish these jobs successfully. The ethical insight associated with each theory and the positions taken by the theory on the ethical assumptions and themes are clues to the kind of ethical job that theory is best suited to address.

Although more than one theory can be useful in helping us live together successfully, not all theories are useful for this purpose. Some theories have problems with one of the first three criteria. Other theories meet the first three criteria but have problems with the fourth. I do not believe that the theories in the first category are useful. If the theory cannot produce ethical guidelines, show that some are better than others, or prohibit the unlimited pursuit of self-interest, it cannot help us live together successfully. However, if a theory does all of these but is not completely successful at helping us solve ethical problems, it can still be useful. Based on this position, we can eliminate ethical subjectivism, ethical relativism, and ethical egoism. We should retain utilitarianism, Kantian ethics, moral rights theory, virtue ethics, and the ethic of care.

Moral Communities and Loyalty

One way to develop the idea of using multiple ethical theories to help us to live together successfully and solve moral problems is by building on Andrew Oldenquist's valuable discussion of moral communities and loyalty.[1] He claims that when I am loyal toward something I have come to view it as mine, yet the object of my loyalty can be shared with other people.[2] Group loyalty toward a common good can define a moral community.

> Our wide and narrow loyalties define moral communities or domains.... A loyalty defines a moral community in terms of a conception of a common good and a special commitment to the members of the group who share this good.[3]

Oldenquist adds that we belong simultaneously to many moral communities, some narrow and others wide. Families, friends, neighborhoods, organizations, corporations, ethnic groups, countries, all human beings, or even all morally significant beings are examples of such communities. The system of moral communities might be represented by drawing concentric circles with the self in the middle and the moral community of all morally significant beings as the outermost circle.

Oldenquist claims that a moral community is a group of persons bound together by loyalty, a vision of a common good, and a special commitment to the members of the group. I accept his view that there are moral communities and that loyalty is often the crucial element that binds a moral community together, but I have reservations about his ideas of a common good and a special commitment to the members of the community. Many moral communities share only a very vague idea of a common good. Pluralistic societies such as the United States no longer share an articulated and clear vision of the common good, even though people living in these societies have definite ideas about what constitutes their individual good. There may be a strong commitment to other members in some moral communities, like families, whereas in other communities, like countries, the commitment to other citizens may be weak. Without a clear vision of the common good and a strong commitment to the other members of the community, how do we live together successfully and solve moral problems? We can use ethical theories to help us answer this question.

With the exception of ethical relativism, the ethical theories discussed in this book do not fit Oldenquist's view that a conception of a common good exists to help define and bind together an actual moral community. Instead, these ethical theories might be described as intellectual or reflective approaches to ethics. The thinkers who created these theories wanted to alter or reject the actual moral considerations that sprang from moral communities. Because the theories did not originate in actual moral communities, they were cut off from the motivating power of loyalty to a community. The theories were ways of thinking about ethics endorsed by certain moral philosophers and those influenced by them. Although the various ethical theories might have influenced individuals within some Western countries, no community has consciously adopted an ethical theory. It is true that the language of rights is used by many governments, particularly in international affairs, but ordinary people in these countries do not make day-to-day, morally significant decisions based on reasoning about rights. Even though ordinary people do not make much use of ethical theories, this does not mean that ethical theories could not be helpful to them. Can ethical theories help people live together successfully and solve moral problems? Oldenquist's ideas provide a clue to a way of thinking about ethics and ethical theories that answers this question in an interesting way. Let's consider this question further.

Full-Scale Morally Significant Beings

The largest moral community is composed of all full-scale morally significant beings. When we interact with persons only as full-scale morally significant beings, we should disregard factors that are irrelevant to this moral status, such as age, gender, and color, and treat them as moral equals. Because these persons are moral equals, an egalitarian ethical theory would be the reasonable moral resource to use to help us live successfully with members of this largest moral community. We have discussed three egalitarian ethical theories—utilitarianism, Kantian ethics, and moral rights theory. How do we choose a theory or theories that will help us live successfully with the members of this community?

If we want to maintain a successful relationship with *all* the members of this community, we should eliminate utilitarianism.[4] Utilitarians act for the greatest good of the greatest number of people and must be willing to sacrifice a minority for the greater good of the majority. If we want to live successfully with all the members of the community, we cannot sacrifice some of them for the good of others. We need a theory that regards all persons as valuable to increase our chances of living successfully with all of them.

The insights and themes show us that both Kantian ethics and the moral rights theory view persons as moral equals who are all valuable. Kantian ethics is related to the insight that persons are moral equals and that our ethical treatment of persons in sufficiently similar situations ought to be consistent. According to proponents of the theory, we must act only from those personal rules that we can at the same time will to be moral laws, and we must also act in regard to all persons in ways that treat them as ends in themselves and never simply as means to accomplish the ends of others. These principles could be used as an ethical guide to help us live more successfully with people in general.

The moral rights theory would also produce a useful set of ethical guidelines. This theory claims that individual persons are valuable and that we need to act in ways that respect their value. Moral rights are used to respect their value by giving persons legitimate claims to protection for their vital interests. Avoiding violations of the moral rights of others would also help us live successfully with these persons.

Both the moral rights theory and Kantian ethics can help us understand our moral obligations to persons who are not part of one of our smaller moral communities. It is in regard to this aspect of ethics that moral equality is essential. We need to protect equally all full-scale morally significant beings, and we need a moral resource to help us do so. Neither of these theories would be a complete success, but both establish a kind of "moral minimum" with regard to persons in general. For practical reasons, I prefer the moral rights theory. Avoiding violations of moral rights seems clearer and more precise to me than acting from those personal rules that a person could will to be moral laws. Choosing between these two theories is not crucial, however, because either one would provide an appropriate moral minimum.

Why should we endorse the moral minimum in regard to full-scale morally significant beings? My answer is a conditional and pragmatic one. If we value a successful connection to other persons, simply as persons, then we should treat them ethically. Egalitarian ethical theories ignore the idea of loyalty to moral communities, but the idea of loyalty can be connected to these theories. If I have some degree of loyalty to persons in general, or to persons with whom I have no close relationship, then I will feel bound by the moral minimum.

Egalitarian ethical theories like utilitarianism, Kantian ethics, and the moral rights theory relate best to the broadest possible moral community: all full-scale morally significant beings. Historically, these theories have tended to elevate moral obligations to this moral community above obligations to other such communities. The proponents of egalitarian ethical theories have emphasized our moral obligations to all full-scale morally significant beings and downgraded our moral relationships to persons who occupy more specific roles (e.g., family members, friends, and neighbors) and who are members of smaller moral communities.

I believe egalitarian ethical theories put too much emphasis on our moral obligations to all full-scale morally significant beings to qualify as our only ethical resource. Because these theories assume that "ethical" is inexorably linked with the moral equality of all full-scale morally significant beings and that general moral obligations always outweigh everything else, they neglect the reality that moral considerations are related to a multiplicity of moral communities.

Oldenquist asks why wider moral communities should take precedence over more narrow ones, and this is a good question. Egalitarian ethical theories need not take precedence over other approaches to ethics related to more narrow moral communities. Egalitarian theories attempt to articulate our moral relationship with persons in general, but they are not the whole of ethics. These theories have an important role to play, but they are only one element in ethical life. They should not necessarily take precedence over everything else.[5]

It is possible, of course, that an egalitarian theory might be the most important ethical resource for an individual whose loyalty and connection to persons in general was greater than his or her loyalty and connection to the members of smaller moral communities. This would tell us something about the person's loyalties, but not something about ethics in general. Developing a pluralistic ethical position allows us to use multiple ethical resources to help us live successfully with the members of various moral communities. It also provides a way to resolve conflicts between competing ethical obligations.

When trying to solve an ethical problem, we need to identify the moral community or communities to which the problem relates and use the ethical resource or theory appropriate to that community. If two communities connected to two different ethical theories are involved, we will need to see if both theories produce the same answer. If they do not, there will be a conflict. I will discuss such conflicts in a later section.

Of the ethical problems mentioned in Chapter 1, only the case involving stealing a book from a bookstore deals with people simply as full-scale morally significant beings. Typically, we have no close relation with the owners and employees of a store; that is, they do not belong to one of our smaller moral communities. Therefore, the appropriate ethical resource for this problem would be the moral rights theory or Kantian ethics. Based on the moral rights theory, it would be unethical to steal the book because it would violate the owner's right to property. There seems to be no problem in this case with describing the action as stealing or with conflicting rights. Kantians would reach a similar conclusion. They would argue that the personal rule connected to stealing the book could not be willed to be a moral law; therefore, acting on such a rule would be unethical.

Large Moral Communities

Once we remove egalitarian ethical theories from their position of ethical dominance, we can develop a more pluralistic approach to ethics. We may have connections and loyalties to a variety of moral communities. We value successful relationships to these communities, and such successful relationships usually depend on our acting in an ethical manner toward the members of the moral community.[6] Therefore, we need some ethical resource to guide our conduct toward each group and to allow us to maintain successful relationships with all of them.

The previous section discussed the largest moral community, all full-scale morally significant beings. Some other moral communities also have a large membership, such as countries and ethnic groups. Some people feel a special connection or loyalty to fellow citizens or to members of the same ethnic group. What binds these communities together besides loyalty? Although Oldenquist suggests a vision of a common good and a commitment to that vision, I suggest that it is a common purpose or goal that is of the greatest ethical relevance. Many people might resist the idea that a country's citizens could believe their nation has a purpose, but it is hard to dismiss the idea out of hand. For example, many citizens of the United States believe that our national purpose is to protect the rights of our citizens, and perhaps also to promote the spread of democratic governments. W. E. B. DuBois wrote about African Americans as having a mission to deliver a spiritual message to the world.[7] If members of these communities really share a purpose, then that purpose is ethically relevant.

Some persons are loyal to and have a connection with one or more of these large communities. A particular person might even value his or her connection and loyalty to one of these large moral communities above connections and loyalties to other moral communities. In contrast, other people may have no connection and loyalty to these large moral communities. These persons should treat other citizens and members of the same ethnic group as full-scale morally significant beings and use one of the egalitarian ethical theories as a moral resource.

If persons within these large moral communities share some purpose or goal, then virtue ethics will be superior to an egalitarian theory as a moral resource. As the essential ethical ideas show, virtue ethics is centered around a purpose or function, whereas the egalitarian theories would not recognize the moral significance of such a purpose. Aristotle's basic human purpose might be replaced with a national or ethnic purpose. If a moral community has a purpose or goal, it can develop a view of a well-lived life in connection with achieving that purpose or goal. Virtues can then be identified that will help achieve that well-lived life, although these virtues will probably not be understood in the way Aristotle conceived of them. Patriotism and civic duty were two virtues related to the United States and democracy, and DuBois talked about racial pride and honesty in connection with African Americans.

I am not sure we can really identify a purpose shared by the members of a large moral community, but even if we can we should not expect a version of virtue ethics to be completely effective at helping us live successfully with the members of these large moral communities. To the extent that the virtues can act as moral guidelines, the theory would provide some assistance, however. Of course, virtue ethics will not provide us with resources to evaluate the basic purpose itself. We will be assuming that the basic purpose is ethical and worthwhile. (A questionable purpose is discussed in a later section on misguided loyalty.) If we value our connections to other citizens and ethnic groups, and if the members of these large moral communities share a purpose, then using virtue ethics as a moral resource will help us to act ethically toward these people and preserve our connection.

None of the ethical problems identified in Chapter 1 deals with persons as members of an ethnic group or as fellow citizens. Therefore, in my view, virtue ethics is not the best theory to use to solve any of these problems, although Aristotle would have provided clear answers for several of them. Based on his ethical ideas, you ought to tell the truth if someone asks you a question, no matter how upset the person may be with you for telling the truth. You ought to care more for the truth than for what other people think of you. If your friend asks you if he or she is being deceived, you should tell your friend the truth. Aristotle identifies stealing as one of the actions that is always evil no matter what emotion accompanies it. He would argue that it would be unethical of you to steal the textbook. Finally, he would reject committing suicide. To kill yourself to escape from suffering or a broken heart is the act of a coward. You ought to be courageous and face hardship.

Intermediate Moral Communities

In addition to these large moral communities, we find intermediate moral communities such as neighborhoods, organizations, institutions, small businesses, and corporations. What will allow us to choose the appropriate ethical theory or resource to use with these communities? The major relevant moral factor, I believe, is that the members of these intermediate moral communities share a common purpose or function. This is particularly appropriate for organizations and corporations because they often have mission statements or statements of purpose. If we have some degree of loyalty to an organization or corporation and value our connection to such a moral community, an ethical resource is needed to help us live successfully with its members. The mission statements can act as goals or purposes that can replace Aristotle's human function as the foundation of a version of virtue ethics. The corporate or organizational mission statements provide a foundation that can be used to create a view of a well-lived life and to identify the practices and virtues that will help to accomplish the corporate or organizational mission. If corporations and organizations have missions or purposes, then virtue ethics would be superior to an egalitarian theory as a moral resource. Virtue ethics is centered around a purpose, whereas egalitarian theory would not recognize the moral significance of such an organizational or corporate purpose. A well-lived life, in the corporate or organizational context, will be one where the person thrives as an individual but also is successful at supporting the corporate or organizational mission. Someone who does not help achieve the corporate or organizational mission but thinks only of him- or herself is often unsuccessful in the context of that community. If we value our memberships in organizations and our jobs, we ought to act ethically toward the members of these communities. Virtue ethics provides a moral resource to help us do this.

Virtue ethics will not be completely successful at helping us live successfully with the members of these moral communities and will not provide the ethical resources to evaluate their shared purposes, but it will provide some assistance. One of the ethical problems from Chapter 1 dealt with an organization or institution, a university. The problem involved whether or not you should cheat on a test. One function (or perhaps *the* function) of a university is to educate students and to evaluate students fairly to determine their educational progress. Honesty is a necessary virtue for achieving this function. Teachers must be honest in assessing their students, and students must be honest in completing the assessment instruments, such as tests and papers. Cheating is dishonest and undermines the function of the university. Therefore, cheating on the test would be unethical.

Small Moral Communities

It would not be appropriate to use an egalitarian ethical theory to help us live successfully with our families and friends. If I treat my family and friends the same way I treat strangers, I will alienate my family and lose my friends. To keep our special connection to the people we love and like, we need a moral resource that will endorse giving these people special consideration. The insight and the essential ethical ideas of the ethic of care indicate that it is the theory best able to justify such special consideration. The ethic of care asserts that I should strive to care for certain people, including my family and close friends. I will give them more attention, concern, and assistance than I would give a person who is a member of a larger moral community. I will try to apprehend their reality and promote their welfare. This endorsement of special treatment for those for whom we care will allow us to maintain our special relationships with family and friends.

Most of the problems mentioned in Chapter 1 dealt with friends or intimates. Because the ethic of care is best equipped to endorse special treatment for such people, it is the appropriate ethical resource to use with these moral communities. To solve problems using this ethic, we must apprehend the other's reality and promote his or her welfare. We must figure out how best to care for all those involved. Noddings's book contains suggestions related to a couple of the questions in Chapter 1. She claims that we ought not to steal and would argue that it is unethical to steal a book from a friend.[8] She also claims that a woman should care more for herself and those she already cares for than for an embryo with whom she has not established a caring relationship. An abortion is not unethical if it is necessary for one to continue to be successful as a one-caring (to oneself and to others).[9]

Solving the other moral problems from Chapter 1 will be more difficult. We must apprehend the reality of the people involved in these situations and try to determine how best to promote their welfare. You should not lie to a friend, but neither should you hurt that person. You should probably try to get the person who is cheating to end the relationship or to be honest about what is going on. A relationship that involves deception on the part of one person is not really in the best interest of either person. In relation to the problem about whether or not to leave your lover for another person, the situation is probably even more difficult. How can you best care for both of these people? Will you now think less of the first person and always regret not entering the new relationship? A proponent of the ethic of care would conclude that you cannot stop caring for the first person, but as long as you continue to care, it would probably be ethical to end the romantic aspect of the relationship and become involved with the new person. Based on the ethic of care, the suicide case seems relatively easy. If you really care for your family and your friends, you will not kill yourself. Suicide usually devastates the family and friends of the person who dies, and this act would be contrary to caring for these people. Finally, consider the case where you ask a friend or family member to kill you after being paralyzed from the neck down. If you really care for this person, you would not put him or her in this position. Doing so does not reflect an appreciation of the other person's reality and a concern for his or her welfare.

The main purpose of ethical theories is to help us live more successfully with others and to solve ethical problems. In the preceding sections I have suggested that the best way to utilize ethical theories to accomplish this purpose is to use different theories for different moral communities. I have sketched out the bare bones of this approach, and I encourage you to try to fill it out. In the next section I turn to the major problem with this pluralistic approach to ethics, the problem of conflicting moral obligations.

Moral Communities and Conflicting Moral Obligations

If we have loyalties to a number of moral communities and are trying to live successfully with the members of all of them, we will encounter cases that involve the members of different communities and that include conflicting moral obligations. Sometimes the different ethical guidelines will create conflicting obligations. At other times we possess limited resources and must decide who will receive them. For example, I have only limited time on a Saturday; should I spend it fixing a house for an impoverished family, working at the office, or taking my children to a baseball game? Each individual must decide whether he or she will act in the name of the good related to family, friends, neighbors, coworkers, ethnic groups, other citizens, persons in general, or some combination of these. How should we arbitrate the competing obligations of these different moral communities?

Two basic kinds of conflicts may arise involving the obligations generated by the ethical theories we employ. First are situations where the conflicting moral obligations of two or more moral communities allow us to act only in accord with one of them. In making this choice, however, we will not violate the ethical guidelines of the other theory. I could spend the day kayaking with a friend or taking my children to a baseball game, but not both. In this situation, either choice seems ethical. In contrast, the second kind of case involves conflicting moral obligations wherein acting in accord with the obligations generated by one community and theory would violate the ethical guidelines of another theory. Taking my family to a baseball game on a Saturday when the other employees at my office are struggling to meet a crucial deadline and need my help may be judged as unethical by these other employees. What should we do in cases of these conflicts?

Using Oldenquist's idea, the conflict might be redescribed as a problem about the proper focus for our greatest loyalty. Human beings have different loyalties and are influenced by the different views of what is ethical related to various moral communities. Is there one group or association that should command our highest loyalty? Should one ethical principle take precedence over the others?

I believe that our relationships to the members of all our moral communities are crucial because these relationships help to define us as individuals. To adapt an idea from Sarah Conly (although I will reach a conclusion different from hers), a person needs a way of life that will allow the person to maintain a general harmony among his or her loyalties to various groups. Without such harmony, the person will not be an integrated individual.[10] Suppose Rose feels loyal to a variety of moral communities: family, friends, women, a corporation, an ethnic group, and persons in general. Instead of making the ethical obligations to the members of one group more important than the others, she might strive to achieve an overall balance among the moral obligations connected to the various moral communities to which she owes some loyalty. Her identity depends on successfully maintaining her ties to all of these groups; therefore, she will not want to sacrifice any of them completely. In an effort to maintain these ties, it is useful for her to act, as much as possible, in accord with all the various ethical guidelines connected to the communities. In cases of conflict she should seek some kind of overall balance. This is not to suggest some absolute equality among the competing obligations; each one must receive what is necessary to maintain the connection. Obligations to family often outweigh obligations connected to an organization, but the demands of the organization must be satisfied to a degree sufficient to maintain the connection. In a particular instance, Rose might weigh the competing claims and decide in favor of the one that would lead to the greatest overall balance among maintaining the connection to all the communities. In one case she might act in accord with the moral rights of persons with whom she has no close relationship, in another because she "cares for" a friend, in a third in accord with the virtue of concern for her customers' satisfaction, and so on. This would allow her to maintain her connection to all of her moral communities. The key is to act in ways that minimize conflict among the various ethical obligations connected to the different moral communities and, when conflicts are inevitable, to try to obtain an overall balance between fulfilling the obligations generated in connection with each group.

This "solution" to the problem of conflicting obligations does not eliminate the conflicts. Instead, it makes a person aware that maintaining the connection to all the moral communities will require an overall balance. It may require moral sensitivity and creativity to identify and achieve this balance, but I believe that doing so is worthwhile. An individual needs connections to a variety of moral communities to live an interesting and fulfilling life. While benefiting from this variety, the individual also needs to create some coherence and harmony among the obligations connected to the different moral communities so that the person can maintain a consistent self-identity. An important part of what a person is results from the relationships in which he or she is involved and the loyalties connected to them.

Misguided Loyalty to a Moral Community

Organizations count as moral communities, but suppose someone belongs to a racist organization whose members regard persons of color as inferior and whose mission is to drive them out of the predominantly white neighborhoods. Based on this mission or purpose, the members of the organization might guide their conduct by a dubious set of "virtues" connected to their mission. They might use intimidation and violence against their victims; they might regard members who are particularly strong and violent as individuals for others to emulate. Based on the ethical guidelines connected to their mission, their conduct would be ethical to them, but most of us would believe they are acting unethically. Are proponents of a pluralistic ethics justified in condemning and trying to stop such conduct?

I have already noted this problem in the discussion of virtue ethics. Although a purpose allows us to ethically evaluate other things, it does not allow us to evaluate the purpose itself. The key to understanding why pluralists see some loyalties as misguided and unethical is that they have adopted an overriding goal or purpose: to try to live successfully with all persons. More specific purposes, such as driving away people of color, that would conflict with this overriding purpose are unethical. Pluralists cannot tolerate conduct that would harm or humiliate persons because it would prevent their living successfully with these persons.[11] Of course, we will not be able to ethically evaluate the overriding pluralistic purpose. The commitment to living successfully with all other persons is ultimately what makes us pluralists. It is simply the ground on which we stand.

Conclusion

I have sketched out a way to use multiple ethical theories to try to help us live successfully with others and to solve moral problems. This pluralistic approach views egalitarian moral theories as important resources but not as the only appropriate ethical resources. We are usually closely tied to our family and friends and need few reminders of their importance to us, but our identification with and loyalty to other persons is often weak. The task of the proponents of egalitarian ethical theories should not merely be to express our universal moral obligations but also to illustrate and strengthen our bonds with persons in the largest community. The moral sensitivity to see our connection with other persons, especially those who are different from us, is the beginning of the formation of new loyalties and connections to moral communities beyond friends and family.

This pluralistic approach to ethics takes for granted the overriding value of attempting to live successfully with all persons. It endorses striving to balance the moral obligations to all the competing moral communities to which we are loyal. Our identities depend on successfully maintaining our ties to all of these groups. Therefore, we must try to minimize conflicts among the various ethical obligations connected to different communities and, in cases where conflict is unavoidable, to seek some kind of overall balance.

I began this chapter by acknowledging that no single ethical theory is completely effective at helping us live successfully with others and solving ethical problems. Nor is ethical pluralism a complete success, but it is an improvement over a single theory for several reasons. First, if we use the theory that fits best with each community rather than only one theory, our chances of living successfully with the members of various moral communities should be improved. A pluralistic approach ought to do a better job of helping us maintain our connections with all of the moral communities. Second, ethical pluralism eliminates some of the problems that plague single theories. Using a pluralistic approach eliminates the Kantian problem with exceptions to moral laws, the moral rights problem with community, the virtue ethics problem with the fundamental human purpose, and the ethic of care problems with an incomplete moral standard and limits on promoting welfare. By eliminating even some of the problems with these theories, ethical pluralism should make it easier for us to solve moral problems. Finally, a pluralistic ethics also has the advantage of pointing out the incredible diversity, richness, and complexity of ethical life. It shows us how being ethical involves many moral communities, including our families, friends, neighborhoods, organizations, corporations, institutions, ethnic groups, and persons in general.

QUESTIONS FOR REVIEW

Here are some questions to help you review the main concepts in this chapter.

1. What is the most important function of ethical theories?

2. According to Oldenquist, what is a moral community? How does loyalty relate to moral communities? What are the problems with accepting Oldenquist's idea of a common good?

3. What ethical theory is the best moral resource to use with full-scale morally significant beings? with large moral communities? with intermediate moral communities? with small moral communities?

4. Is utilitarianism the best theory to use with full-scale morally significant beings? Why, or why not? Support your position.

5. What is the ethical pluralist position regarding egalitarian theories? How is this view different from the one endorsed by most of the proponents of egalitarian theories?

6. How can we resolve moral conflicts among the contending moral obligations connected to different moral communities?

7. Discuss the difference between a dispute involving the moral obligations related to two moral communities and a conflict involving the moral obligations connected to a moral community and self-interest? To be ethical, must we sometimes sacrifice our self-interest? Why, or why not?

8. What is the overall purpose underlying ethical pluralism? How does this purpose help us identify misguided loyalties?

9. Do you feel loyalty or a special connection to the members of any of these moral communities? Why?

10. Choose one of the moral problems identified in Chapter 1 and explain how a pluralistic ethics would solve that problem. Why would a pluralistic ethics solve it in this way?

11. Is ethical pluralism an improvement over using a single ethical theory? Support your answer with examples from your own experience.

NOTES

1. In his paper entitled "Loyalties," Andrew Oldenquist develops the ideas of moral communities and loyalty and their importance for ethics. This chapter was strongly influenced by Oldenquist, although my conclusions differ from his. See Andrew Oldenquist, "Loyalties," *The Journal of Philosophy,* 1982, 79: 173–193.

2. Ibid., 175.

3. Ibid., 177.

4. Some readers will believe that I have too quickly dismissed utilitarianism. For me, the willingness to sacrifice a minority for the good of the majority is the most significant difference between utilitarian and deontological theories. Because I believe in trying to live successfully with all persons, I cannot endorse sacrificing some of them. I also have serious practical concerns about utilitarianism. Act and rule utilitarianism are not successful at solving problems whose consequences are impossible or very difficult to predict. The abortion case mentioned in Chapter 1, for example, could not be solved using a utilitarian theory. It is impossible to predict the consequences because we would have to know what harm and benefit would result if the fetus were allowed to live. Would the resulting person grow up to invent a cure for cancer or become a mass murderer? These determinations are impossible to make; therefore, utilitarianism cannot be used to solve such moral problems. Even in a case where utilitarian theory would seem to work much better, I still have concerns. Regarding the problems connected to cheating on a test or stealing a book, a person should be able to predict with reasonable accuracy the harms and benefits for everyone produced by each outcome. The problem, of course, is to predict the probability of being caught. I am not sure we can ever accurately make these predictions. In the case where a person has been paralyzed, this person

thinks that he or she can predict the future with great accuracy—a life filled with pain and humiliation--—but is this really correct? I appreciate the insight connected to utilitarianism, but I do not feel comfortable using the theory to solve ethical problems.

5. I first encountered this idea that ethical theories were only one aspect of moral life in Lawrence Blum, *Friendship, Altruism and Morality* (Boston: Routledge & Kegan Paul, 1980).

6. What constitutes a successful relationship between an individual and a moral community is a difficult notion, although I think it can be spelled out in a way that is neither subjective nor relative. My strategy would be to develop the idea that certain objective values are connected to specific practices essential to moral communities. These values are internal to the community and do not apply outside it, but they still have a strong objective component. The arguments required to establish this conclusion are beyond the scope of this chapter.

7. W. E. B. DuBois, "The Conservation of Races," in *The Oxford W. E. B. DuBois Reader,* edited by Eric J. Sundquist (New York: Oxford University Press, 1996).

8. Nel Noddings, *Caring: A Feminine Approach to Ethics and Moral Education* (Berkeley: University of California Press, 1984), p. 93.

9. Ibid., pp. 87–89.

10. Sarah Conly, "The Objectivity of Morals and the Subjectivity of Agents," *American Philosophical Quarterly,* 1985, 22: 281.

11. An ethical pluralist can, of course, harm others in self-defense. We should try to live successfully with everyone, but if others threaten our lives, we must defend ourselves and may be forced to harm them.

Appendix 1

Insights

Ethical Relativism	A legitimate set of ethical guidelines is related to an actual society or group.
Act Utilitarianism	An action is morally bad if it harms someone, whereas it is morally good if it helps or benefits someone.
Kantian Ethics	Persons are moral equals, and our ethical treatment of persons in sufficiently similar situations ought to be consistent.
Moral Rights Theory	Individual persons are valuable, and we should act in ways that respect their value.
Virtue Ethics	The virtues help persons achieve well-being or live good lives.
Ethic of Care	Ethics is primarily concerned with relationships between persons.

Traditional Assumptions

ASPECTS OF THE TRADITIONAL ETHICAL ASSUMPTIONS

Ethical Theories	*Is ethics rational?*	*Are people moral equals?*	*Can we universalize some ethical evaluations?*
Ethical Relativism	Yes	No	Yes (No)
Act Utilitarianism	Yes	Yes	Yes
Kantian Ethics	Yes	Yes	Yes
Moral Rights Theory	Yes	Yes	Yes
Virtue Ethics	Yes	No	Yes
Ethic of Care	No	No	No

Themes

Ethical Theories	Are some actions, beliefs and values always either good or evil?	Should we focus on consequences or reasoning?	Should we focus on rules or actions?	Should we focus on the group or the individual?
Ethical Relativism	No	Reasoning	Rules	Group
Act Utilitarianism	Yes	Consequences	Actions	Group
Kantian Ethics	Yes	Reasoning	Rules	Individual
Moral Rights Theory	Yes	Reasoning	Rules	Individual
Virtue Ethics	Yes	Both	Neither	Both
Ethic of Care	Yes	Consequences	Actions	Individual

Appendix 2

The United Nations Universal Declaration of Human Rights, 1948

Preamble

Whereas recognition of the inherent dignity and of the equal and inalienable rights of all members of the human family is the foundation of freedom, justice and peace in the world,

Whereas disregard and contempt for human rights have resulted in barbarous acts which have outraged the conscience of mankind, and the advent of a world in which human beings shall enjoy freedom of speech and belief and freedom from fear and want has been proclaimed as the highest aspiration of the common people,

Whereas it is essential, if man is not to be compelled to have recourse, as a last resort, to rebellion against tyranny and oppression, that human rights should be protected by the rule of law,

Whereas it is essential to promote the development of friendly relations between nations,

Whereas the people of the United Nations have in the Charter reaffirmed their faith in fundamental human rights, in the dignity and worth of the human person and in the equal rights of men and women and have determined to promote social progress and better standards of life in larger freedom,

Whereas Member States have pledged themselves to achieve, in cooperation with the United Nations, the promotion of universal respect for and observance of human rights and fundamental freedoms,

Whereas a common understanding of these rights and freedoms is of the greatest importance for the full realization of this pledge,

Now, therefore,

The General Assembly Proclaims

This Universal Declaration of Human Rights as a common standard of achievement for all peoples and all nations, to the end that every individual and every organ of society, keeping this Declaration constantly in mind, shall strive by teaching and education to promote respect for these rights and freedoms and by progressive measures, national and international, to secure their universal and effective recognition and observance, both among the peoples of Member States themselves and among the peoples of territories under their jurisdiction.

Article 1 All human beings are born free and equal in dignity and rights. They are endowed with reason and conscience and should act towards one another in a spirit of brotherhood.

Article 2 Everyone is entitled to all the rights and freedoms set forth in this Declaration, without distinction of any kind, such as race, colour, sex, language, religion, political or other opinion, national or social origin, property, birth or other status.

Furthermore, no distinction shall be made on the basis of the political, jurisdictional or international status of the country or territory to which a person belongs, whether it be independent, trust, non-self-governing or under any other limitation of sovereignty.

Article 3 Everyone has the right to life, liberty and security of person.

Article 4 No one shall be held in slavery or servitude; slavery and the slave trade shall be prohibited in all their forms.

Article 5 No one shall be subjected to torture or to cruel, inhuman or degrading treatment or punishment.

Article 6 Everyone has the right to recognition everywhere as a person before the law.

Article 7 All are equal before the law and are entitled without any discrimination to equal protection of the law. All are entitled to equal protection against any discrimination in violation of this Declaration and against any incitement to such discrimination.

Article 8 Everyone has the right to an effective remedy by the competent national tribunals for acts violating the fundamental rights granted him by the constitution or by law.

Article 9 No one shall be subjected to arbitrary arrest, detention or exile.

Article 10 Everyone is entitled in full equality to a fair and public hearing by an independent and impartial tribunal, in the determination of his rights and obligations and of any criminal charge against him.

Article 11 1. Everyone charged with a penal offence has the right to be presumed innocent until proved guilty according to law in a public trial at which he has had all the guarantees necessary for his defence.
2. No one shall be held guilty of any penal offence on account of any act or omission which did not constitute a penal offence, under national or international law, at the time when it was committed. Nor shall a heavier penalty be imposed than the one that was applicable at the time the penal offence was committed.

Article 12 No one shall be subjected to arbitrary interference with his privacy, family, home or correspondence, nor to attacks upon his honour and reputation. Everyone has the right to the protection of the law against such interference or attacks.

Article 13 1. Everyone has the right to freedom of movement and residence within the borders of each state.
2. Everyone has the right to leave any country, including his own, and to return to his country.

Article 14 1. Everyone has the right to seek and to enjoy in other countries asylum from persecution.
2. This right may not be invoked in the case of prosecutions genuinely arising from non-political crimes or from acts contrary to the purposes and principles of the United Nations.

Article 15 1. Everyone has the right to a nationality.
2. No one shall be arbitrarily deprived of his nationality nor denied the right to change his nationality.

Article 16 1. Men and women of full age, without any limitation due to race, nationality or religion, have the right to marry and to found a family. They are entitled to equal rights as to marriage, during marriage and at its dissolution.
2. Marriage shall be entered into only with the free and full consent of the intending spouses.
3. The family is the natural and fundamental group unit of society and is entitled to protection by society and the State.

Article 17 1. Everyone has the right to own property alone as well as in association with others.

2. No one shall be arbitrarily deprived of his property.

Article 18 Everyone has the right to freedom of thought, con-science and religion; this right includes freedom to change his religion or belief, and freedom, either alone or in community with others and in public or private, to manifest his religion or belief in teaching, practice, worship and observance.

Article 19 Everyone has the right to freedom of opinion and expres-sion; this right includes freedom to hold opinions without interference and to seek, receive and impart information and ideas through any media and regardless of frontiers.

Article 20 1. Everyone has the right to freedom of peaceful assem-bly and association.
2. No one may be compelled to belong to an association.

Article 21 1. Everyone has the right to take part in the government of his country, directly or through freely chosen representatives.
2. Everyone has the right of equal access to public service in his country.
3. The will of the people shall be the basis of the authority of gov-ernment; this will shall be expressed in periodic and genuine elections which shall be by universal and equal suffrage and shall be held by secret vote or by equivalent free voting procedures.

Article 22 Everyone, as a member of society, has the right to social security and is entitled to realization, through national effort and inter-national co-operation and in accordance with the organization and resources of each State, of the economic, social and cultural rights indis-pensable for his dignity and the free development of his personality.

Article 23 1. Everyone has the right to work, to free choice of employment, to just and favourable conditions of work and to protec-tion against unemployment.
2. Everyone, without any discrimination, has the right to equal pay for equal work.
3. Everyone who works has the right to just and favourable remu-neration ensuring for himself and his family an existence worthy of human dignity, and supplemented, if necessary, by other means of social protection.
4. Everyone has the right to form and to join trade unions for the protection of his interests.

Article 24 Everyone has the right to rest and leisure, including reasonable limitation of working hours and periodic holidays with pay.

Article 25 1. Everyone has the right to a standard of living adequate for the health and well-being of himself and of his family, including food, clothing, housing and medical care and necessary social services, and the right to security in the event of unemployment, sickness, disability, widowhood, old age or other lack of livelihood in circumstances beyond his control.

2. Motherhood and childhood are entitled to special care and assistance. All children, whether born in or out of wedlock, shall enjoy the same social protection.

Article 26 1. Everyone has the right to education. Education shall be free, at least in the elementary and fundamental stages. Elementary education shall be compulsory. Technical and professional education shall be made generally available and higher education shall be equally accessible to all on the basis of merit.

2. Education shall be directed to the full development of the human personality and to the strengthening of respect for human rights and fundamental freedoms. It shall promote understanding, tolerance and friendship among all nations, racial, or religious groups, and shall further the activities of the United Nations for the maintenance of peace.

3. Parents have a prior right to choose the kind of education that shall be given to their children.

Article 27 1. Everyone has the right freely to participate in the cultural life of the community, to enjoy the arts and to share in scientific advancement and its benefits.

2. Everyone has the right to the protection of the moral and material interests resulting from any scientific, literary or artistic production of which he is the author.

Article 28 Everyone is entitled to a social and international order in which the rights and freedoms set forth in this Declaration can be fully realized.

Article 29 1. Everyone has duties to the community in which alone the free and full development of his personality is possible.

2. In the exercise of his rights and freedoms, everyone shall be subject only to such limitations as are determined by law solely for the purpose of securing due recognition and respect for the rights and freedoms of others and of meeting the just requirements of morality, public order and the general welfare in a democratic society.

3. These rights and freedoms may in no case be exercised contrary to the purposes and principles of the United Nations.

Article 30   Nothing in this Declaration may be interpreted as implying for any State, group or person any right to engage in any activity or to perform any act aimed at the destruction of any of the rights and freedoms set forth herein.

Index

act utilitarianism, 9, 12, 31, 33–46,
    48–49, 60, 65, 74–75, 77, 112, 113
  calculations, 37–39
  ethical standard of, 33
  and the ethical themes, 40–41
  justification of, 35–36
  and moral significance, 36
  problems with, 42–46
  related ethical insight, 31
  and the traditional ethical
      assumptions, 39–40
Aristotle, 81–93, 115, 116
attitudes, 4–5

Bentham, Jeremy, 33, 36, 38–39, 66,
    67, 72

Conly, Sarah, 119
consequentialist ethical theories, 31,
    46
  See also ethical consequentialism
cultural relativism, 17–18, 20

deontological ethical theories, 52, 74
  See also deontology
deontology, 11, 52
DuBois, W. E. B., 114–115

emotions, 84–86
ethical assumptions, 7–10
  and act utilitarianism, 39–40
  and ethical relativism, 21–22
  and the ethic of care, 101
  and Kantian ethics, 58–59
  and moral rights theory, 72–73
  and virtue ethics, 87–88
ethical consequentialism, 11–12,
    40–41
ethical egoism, 31–33, 110
ethical insights, 109
  insight related to ethical relativism,
      15
  insight related to the ethic of care,
      97
  insight related to Kantian ethics, 52
  insight related to moral rights
      theory, 65
  insight related to utilitarianism, 31
  insight related to virtue ethics, 81
ethical objectivism, 11, 14
ethical pluralism, 109–122
ethical relativism, 15, 17–29, 41–42,
    111

ethical standard of, 18
  and the ethical themes, 22–23
  justification of, 20–21
  and moral significance, 21
  problems with, 23–28
  related ethical insight, 15
  and tolerance, 18–20
  and the traditional ethical
      assumptions, 21–22
ethical subjectivism, 15–17
ethical themes, 10–13
  and act utilitarianism, 40–41
  and ethical relativism, 22–23
  and the ethic of care, 101–102
  and Kantian ethics, 59–60
  and moral rights theory, 73–74
  and virtue ethics, 88–89
ethical theories, 3, 5–13, 22, 31,
    109–113, 121–122
  egalitarian, 9, 112–113
  evaluation of, 6–7
  nonegalitarian, 9
ethic of care, 95–106, 117–118
  ethical caring, 97–100
  ethical standard of, 99
  and the ethical themes, 101–102
  justification of, 100–101
  and moral significance, 100
  natural caring, 97–98
  problems with, 103–105
  related ethical insight, 97
  and the traditional ethical
      assumptions, 101
ethics, 2, 11–13, 34, 96–97, 121–122
  applied ethics, 2–3
  theoretical ethics, 2–3

Gilligan, Carol, 95–97, 105

Hahn, Norma, 96
happiness, 33, 34

injustice, 44–45

Kantian ethical theory, 9, 51–63, 112,
    113
  and the Categorical Imperative,
      54–55
  ethical standard of, 54–55
  and the ethical themes, 59–60
  justification of, 57–58
  and moral laws, 53–54, 55–57

Kantian ethical theory *(continued)*
  and moral significance, 58
  problems with, 60–62
  related ethical insights, 52
  and rules, 52
  and the traditional ethical
    assumptions, 39–40
Kant, Immanuel, 12, 51, 52, 54, 58, 61,
  62, 78
Kohlberg, Lawrence, 95–96, 105

laws, 4–5, 21, 51
Locke, John, 66, 67, 68, 70
loyalty, 110–112, 114, 115, 119, 120,
  122
  misguided, 120–121

Marx, Karl, 77
Midgley, Mary, 5
Mill, John Stuart, 33, 38, 39–40, 44
moral agents, 7–8, 33, 36, 40
moral communities, 110–111, 118–121
  and conflicting moral obligations,
    118–120
  full-scale morally significant beings,
    111–114
  intermediate, 116–117
  large, 114–116
  misguided loyalty to, 120–121
  small, 117–118
moral equality, 8–10
  and act utilitarianism, 39–40
  and ethical relativism, 22
  and the ethic of care, 101
  and Kantian ethics, 52–53, 59
  and moral rights, 73
  and virtue ethics, 87
morality, 20, 21, 22, 26
moral luck, 45–46, 91–92
morally significant beings, 9–10, 36, 66
  full-status morally significant beings,
    9–10, 36–37, 66–67, 111–114
  second-class morally significant
    beings, 9–10, 36–37, 66–67
moral responsibility, 7
  criteria for, 7–8
moral rights, 65–67, 71–78
  entitlement rights, 71–72
  protection rights, 67, 72
  right to liberty, 69
  right to life, 68
  right to privacy, 69–70
  right to property, 70–71
  right to well-being, 68–69
moral rights theory, 9, 65–78, 89–90,
  112

ethical standard of, 67
  and the ethical themes, 73–74
  justification of, 72
  and moral significance, 72
  problems with, 75–78
  related ethical insight, 65
  and the traditional ethical
    assumptions, 72–73

Noddings, Nel, 95–106, 117

Oldenquist, Andrew, 110–111, 113,
  114, 119

pleasure, 33, 34, 40

rationality, 7–8
relationships, 4, 97–100, 101, 104, 106,
  117, 119, 120
religion, 3–4
rule utilitarianism, 12, 46–48, 56

sentiments, 97–98, 101
Singer, Peter, 36
Stevenson, Charles, 15–17

universalizability, 10, 22, 40, 59, 73,
  88, 101
utilitarianism, 33, 111–112
  See also act utilitarianism and rule
    utilitarianism
utility, 33

value, 35
  instrumental value, 35
  intrinsic value, 35–36
vices, 84, 88
virtue, 3, 78, 84–86, 88, 116
virtue ethics, 81–93, 102–103, 115, 116
  ethical standard of, 83–86
  and the ethical themes, 88–89
  justification of, 86
  and moral significance, 86–87
  problems with, 90–92
  related ethical insight, 81
  and the traditional ethical
    assumptions, 87–88
virtues, 81–82, 86–93, 115, 116
  intellectual virtues, 83–84
  moral virtues, 84–86

Warren, Mary Anne, 36, 66, 67
Williams, Bernard, 19–20